Growing Together

A three-part guide for following Jesus
and bringing friends on the journey

Funding for this research was made possible by the generous support of The Navigators. Barna Group was solely responsible for data collection, analysis and writing of the report.

Table of Contents

Preface

by PATRIECE JOHNSON of *The Navigators*

I can say with confidence that reading this book could be life-changing for you and the people you care about. I know it's a bold statement, but I'm certain that's what will happen, if you let it.

Why? Because decades ago, when I was first exposed to the truths about discipleship shared here and let them sink into my heart and influence my priorities, I experienced a new level of transformation from Gods' grace and power in my life. When that happens—and I've seen it happen again and again in friends' lives since—everything changes for the better, including our capacity to endure the hardest of times.

I remember sitting in the dorm room of my Christian university as a freshman, crying out to God, "There has to be more to Christianity than just filling my mind with knowledge and arguing different theological perspectives!"

I wanted my faith to make a difference in the world. I wanted the deep and personal relationship with Jesus that I'd said "yes" to and hadn't (yet) experienced as powerfully as I'd hoped.

God heard my prayer and, in his love, put me on a new course. He brought women into my life through The Navigators whose commitment to me reflected 1 Thessalonians 2:8: "Because we loved you so much, we were delighted to share with you not only the gospel of God but our lives as well." I came to learn that's the essence of something The Navigators call Life-to-Life discipleship: being committed not only to following and sharing about Jesus, but also to investing time in friends, family, coworkers or neighbors to help them do the same, wherever they are on their spiritual journeys.

This was exactly what my soul was longing for! The missing, personal and purposeful link in my spiritual journey.

Is it missing from your journey as well? If so, dig into these pages! You won't regret it.

For 90 years, Navigators have helped people around the world bring hope and purpose to others through something we call "Life-to-Life" discipleship. It's not a program or curriculum, it's more of a commitment to help our friends know Jesus, starting from wherever they are in life.

Life-to-Life discipleship has three layers to it: "To know Christ, make him known and help others do the same."

This means that wherever we are, Navigators are helping people to:

- Share the gospel of Jesus Christ with those who don't yet know him
- Help their friends grow in relationship with God through study of the Word and prayer
- Equip those we disciple to invest their own lives in discipling others

Navigators are investing in others on college campuses, military bases, in cities, neighborhoods and workplaces, as well as in hard-to-reach places all over the world.

To learn more about how you can grow in your faith and help others do the same, visit us at **navigators.org**.

One of the most powerful lessons I've learned about discipleship is that it's more of a lifestyle than a program. The women who have invested in me over the years have been busy wives and moms who often worked full-time, so the time they spent discipling me was very organic to who they were. We met regularly to process life and talk about our walks with Jesus at soccer games or at playgrounds while their children played. We found time to pray and read the Bible together when we could. They walked with me through real-life circumstances—the hard and the beautiful—which, when you think about it, is exactly what Jesus did with his disciples.

This model of discipleship is so empowering to all of us, because it gives us space to be creative, to be flexible, to be us. The everyday choices you make have a ripple effect on whatever families and communities you are a part of.

In *Growing Together: A Three-Part Guide for Following Jesus and Bringing Friends on the Journey*, you'll find some surprising statistics and some powerful testimonies from everyday folks who are seeing God do awesome things just because they're showing up, ready and willing to see if gospel hope really can flow through them to friends, neighbors, coworkers and family.

I pray that the first part is a quick and stirring read that ignites a yearning in your heart for the powerful blessing of discipleship. I trust that the second part will help light the path ahead with some practical, doable advice for all of us who are leading busy lives that don't seem to have margin in them for "something new." And I pray part three will inspire you toward courageous, compassionate conversations—and reassure you that you have what it takes to disciple others in the way of Jesus.

At a time when headlines and conversations online make it seem like any faith conviction has the potential to be polarizing, discipleship returns us to the way Jesus himself most often talked about the hope of the gospel—by walking alongside his disciples and inviting them to live life with him, become like him and embrace his mission. If the gospel is true, and I am fully convinced that it is, there is no better way to love someone than to have the courage to offer them this.

That little freshman girl crying out to God in her dorm room was longing for something real, something powerful, something personal. And that is exactly what she got. It's exactly what our world is crying out for. It is the need of the hour. Through it, we can pass on to others, one life at a time, what has been passed on to us.

Let *Growing Together* speak to your heart. May it help you move forward with confidence that God can use your life to transform the lives of those around you—not because you are up to the task, but because he is. Remember, it's not your ability, but your availability to God's purposes in you and through you, that matters most.

Patriece Johnson
Navigators City Director, Cincinnati

Introduction

by DAVID KINNAMAN of *Barna Group*

Friend and fellow disciple,

It's a hard time in our society to follow Jesus, isn't it?

This is more than a hunch for me. I know this because our team at Barna Group has been tracking data on the intersection of faith and culture for nearly four decades now. The facts tell a sobering story: Most people in our society are moving away from Christianity.

Even more, we're living in a world I call "digital Babylon."

Our "digital Babylon" is a culture marked by phenomenal *access* (thanks, Wi-Fi everywhere), profound *alienation* (from institutions and traditions that give structure and meaning to our lives) and a crisis of *authority* (which, like institutions and traditions, is increasingly viewed with suspicion). How do we find the path that leads to real, worthwhile wisdom for living well and following Jesus in this accelerated, complex culture?

Church history reminds us that living faithfully has never been easy. Certainly, God's people have weathered hostile seasons in the past. But our research shows that resilient faith is very tough to grow today. We need new habits and practices if we're going to build a faith that can stand the test of time—especially *these* times.

Christians are and always have been exiles, people living as strangers in their own land. We need to build a faith that can withstand intense cultural forces to become fully formed disciples of Jesus with a faith worth sharing.

The fact that you're holding this book and plan to use it as a tool to help sustain and nurture your faith means that you're likely among the resilient disciples—a faithful exile looking for practical ways to overcome the challenges of living as a Christian in a world that too often devalues faith.

This book offers you practical ways to make your faith part of your everyday life. It'll help you confront indifference and apathy—two forces that are always pulling at us and causing us to ask, why does discipleship matter anyway? What difference does faith make? How can I make time for church and spiritual growth in my already maxed out schedule? These are real questions that all of us ask. *These are questions that I ask!*

In partnering with The Navigators on this research, I am thrilled that Barna can help equip you to move forward in your faith as a disciple and even a disciplemaker.

This book is designed to serve as a tool to help you confront the obstacles you'll face as you dive deeper into your faith. If you've been traveling solo in your faith, I encourage you to find people who can join you on your journey.

The research in Part 1: How Discipleship Can Transform Your Life attests to the value of having healthy, challenging friendships that fuel a passion for following Jesus. We were never meant to walk alone in our faith. In fact, your spiritual growth is connected to growing with others.

The research in Part 2: What Day-to-Day Discipleship Can Look Like makes me think about how resilient discipleship isn't just good for our faith; it's good for our whole lives. It's a better way to live and to steward our time, energy, influence and relationships. It looks like using our hours well, leaning on one another and staying mindful of the ways God wants to work in our daily lives.

The research in Part 3: Why You're More Ready Than You Think for Disciplemaking shows the fears most people feel about sharing the gospel. Spiritual conversations require humility, empathy and vulnerability. The pages in this book will help you evaluate areas where you can both grow as a disciple of Christ and help others deepen their faith life too.

As you put into practice what you learn inside this book, may you be empowered to push through barriers to build a lasting relationship with God and a faith worth sharing with others.

While we may be living in an unprecedented era—with especially challenging forces pushing our faith—I believe our faith can grow particularly strong in these complex times.

In a time of exile, we find our heart's true home in the Lord.

David Kinnaman

CEO of Barna Group

You Are Here

Chances are, you are hungry to grow closer to God and to further develop your own faith. You would also like to share your faith with others, and you feel it's rewarding to see others grow spiritually. Maybe you've already found yourself in such relationships, and you'd like to learn more about how they work and how you can show up well in them.

On a broader scale, you're the type of person who wants to lean into your faith community and your capacity to have a positive influence on others. This shows up in a willingness to engage with a church, whether in person or online during the pandemic era. You also occasionally practice and nurture your Christianity beyond the typical service, through groups, resources, volunteering, conferences and more.

Now you're looking for a more relational, day-to-day experience of walking with Jesus while walking with others, and you're wondering where to begin.

Barna Group and our project partner The Navigators have been paying close attention to Christians just like you in our research. The paragraphs above summarize some of the beliefs and behaviors of this book's intended audience: committed Christians with the desire and potential to enter meaningful relationships in which people intentionally become more like Christ, together.

We know there can be obstacles to getting started—or that the anxiety surrounding imagined obstacles can become a barrier on its own.

What if I don't have the answers to questions about my faith?

What if I can't make the time?

What if I'm just not the right person to do this?

What if I don't know how to be open with others?

What is the point, anyway?

Other disciples and potential disciplemakers, as we'll refer to them, have pointed to concerns and questions just like these in our surveys. You're not alone. You're also in the right spot.

Each of the three parts of **Growing Together is designed to help you follow Jesus and bring friends on the journey.**

Usually, when we talk about being or making disciples, we're referring to a mutual investment that draws Christians closer to

Barna Group is a research firm dedicated to providing actionable insights on faith and culture, with a particular focus on the Christian Church. In its 35-year history, Barna has conducted more than two million interviews in the course of hundreds of studies and has become a go-to source for organizations that want to better understand a complex and changing world from a faith perspective.

barna.com

God through shared prayer, study, mentoring and up-close-and-personal exposure to how faith works in the lives of people you know and love. Our partner, The Navigators, fittingly calls this Life-to-Life discipleship.

Each of the three sections in *Growing Together* covers an important phase of your journey to draw closer to God and to the people in your life:

- Part 1: How Discipleship Can Transform Your Life
- Part 2: What Day-to-Day Discipleship Can Look Like
- Part 3: Why You're More Ready Than You Think for Disciplemaking

This book is grounded in research from studies Barna has conducted. Yes, that means there will be statistics. If you're a data nerd, enjoy! But just as you don't need to be a pastor or "professional Christian" to help others follow Jesus, you don't need to be a statistician or even all that savvy with numbers to benefit from the key research findings. (If you do want some help, refer to Pointers for Reading Data on page 131.)

Extending the metaphor of a journey, the data act as mile-markers and signposts along the way. We hope they lend clarity and confidence to your experience as a reader, while also providing directions for the twists and turns of growing as a disciple and disciplemaker.

Ultimately, your journey in discipleship is your own—unique to your context, background, relationships and God-given calling. Our research sheds light on those who have gone before you, what we can learn from them and where you are relative to the journeys of other disciples and disciplemakers. Along the way, you'll see question prompts and find stories and insights from some of your peers. **With statistics, stories and opportunities for self-reflection, *Growing Together* is meant to be carried around, marked up and even passed along.**

We'll send you forward now with words from Matthew 28:19–20, known as the Great Commission. In it, Jesus urges and encourages:

"Therefore, go and make disciples of all nations, baptizing them in the name of the Father and of the Son and of the Holy Spirit, and teaching them to obey everything I have commanded you. And surely, I am with you always, to the very end of the age."

The Message version revises this slightly, reminding you that Jesus will "be with you as you do this, day after day after day, right up to the end of the age."

Day after day. Bad and good. Right there in the thick of your routines, your to-do lists, your social circles, your questions, your setbacks, your triumphs. Right up to the end.

PART 1:

How Discipleship Can Transform Your Life

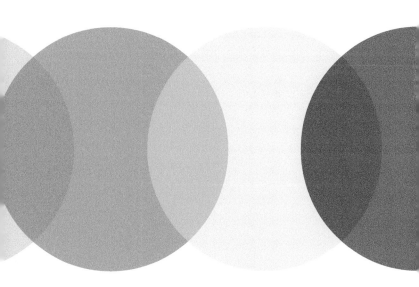

Sharing the Journey

**What we know about the power of pursuing
Jesus together—and what gets in the way**

In the second chapter of the Bible, God sees Adam walking in the Garden of Eden alone. "It is not good for man to be alone," God says (Genesis 2:18).

Later, in the life of Jesus Christ, God in the flesh (John 1:14), we see his commitment to sharing life with others—especially his disciples. "This is my commandment, that you love one another as I have loved you. Greater love has no one than this, that someone lay down his life for his friends. You are my friends," Jesus tells his disciples (John 15:12–14).

Discipleship, a journey of growth toward Christlikeness, is inevitably and intimately connected to the growth of others. As Jesus said, "Where two or three gather in my name, there am I with them" (Matthew 18:20).

Yet while Jesus left a legacy of walking with God in communion with others, many Christians are still traveling solo.

> "We weren't created to do life alone.
> As you grow in Christ,
> bring others on the journey."

Does this statement inspire you?

As you've picked up this book, it likely does! Still, Barna research shows you may be among a minority of Christians.

In a recent Barna survey, only one in three Christians (34%) says this statement is "very" emotionally compelling. Another 41 percent call it "somewhat" compelling, a mostly lukewarm response from the plurality of Christians. Even among the many who consider spiritual growth "very" important (40% of Christians), two in five prefer to pursue growth on their own, privately (41%).

As our society becomes increasingly digital, secular, impersonal and transactional—all existing shifts that have gained momentum in the COVID era—**Christians are challenged anew to appreciate the importance of investing in and receiving from other Christ-followers through discipleship.**

Defining Discipleship

You might be wondering: *What exactly constitutes a discipleship relationship? How do I know if I'm part of one of these relationships?*

It's not a one-size-fits-all connection, but Barna research reveals a couple key ways discipling occurs.

First, we asked respondents whether they have a relationship with someone (other than a family member) that provides all three of these things:

- you hold each other accountable,
- you offer each other encouragement and support, and
- you help each other to grow spiritually.

We'll speak of this as **being discipled** or **being in a discipleship relationship.**

When discipleship is understood in these terms, over half of Christians (56%) say they have a relationship like this. Demographically, Gen Z and Millennials are more likely than older generations to be in a discipleship relationship, while more Black adults (72%) than Hispanic (63%), Asian (57%) or white adults (50%) are in such relationships. These demographic patterns are consistent as we explore discipleship: Younger Christians and racial and ethnic minority groups in the Church are inclined toward a vibrant, social experience of spirituality.

Looking across all adults, this means a slight majority of Christians is sharing accountability, support and spiritual growth with someone else. Still, a sizeable 44 percent of U.S. Christians do *not* say they have a relationship like this in their life.

Barna also asked about and defined **discipling others**—that is, when a Christian specifies that they currently and actively help someone else grow in faith and move closer to Christ. One-third of Christians (33%) is leading this kind of relational investment, which we could also call being a **"disciplemaker."** Again, younger Christians (42% Gen Z, 49% Millennials, 32% Gen X, 19% Boomers) and non-white Christians (53% Black, 39% Hispanic, 33% Asian, 26% white) are more likely than their peers to fall into this category.

Combined, we see more than one-quarter of Christians (28%) experiences *both* of the relationship dynamics described above, and we'll think of them as being members of **discipleship community**. They show signs of being in discipleship relationships *and* they are actively prioritizing helping others grow spiritually.

Some Christians seem to be engaged in just one direction of discipleship. Twenty-eight percent of Christians who are being discipled are not helping someone else grow closer to Christ. On the other hand, it's statistically rare that a Christian would be making disciples without being discipled themselves. Just 5 percent of Christians fall into this category, so we won't always analyze this

The Spectrum of Discipleship Community

● In discipleship community   ● Only discipling others
● Only being discipled   ● Not engaged in discipleship

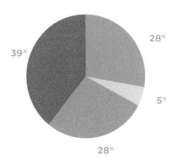

n=2,511 U.S. Christian adults, December 22, 2020–January 18, 2021.

Discipleship Community, by Generation

● In discipleship community ○ Only discipling others
● Only being discipled ● Not engaged in discipleship

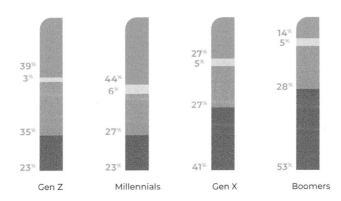

n=2,511 U.S. Christian adults, December 22, 2020–January 18, 2021.

group. Still, their small sample size alone is telling of the give-and-take environment in which discipleship thrives.

Findings like these pose their own questions:

Should we be focused on celebrating the Christians who are walking in a biblical, relational path toward Christlikeness?

Should we be focused on concerns over the Christians who are not presently experiencing discipleship with others?

Yes. And yes.

To encourage or enter these relationships ourselves, we must appreciate when and how they occur. And we must understand why some Christians are not involved in them.

Spiritual Return on Investment

Early research for this project revealed some of the primary reasons Christians, regardless of their generation, have interest in discipling others. Their top motivations were to grow closer to God and to further develop their own faith. Maybe you can relate to these sentiments.

Encouragingly, this study shows that is *exactly* the outcome many Christians are experiencing through their disciplemaking efforts. Christians in discipleship community are more likely to feel re-energized by time spent with Jesus and derive deep joy and satisfaction from their relationship to him.

They also see a stronger connection between their spiritual life and their day-to-day life. About three in five strongly agree their relationship with Jesus impacts the way they live their life every day.

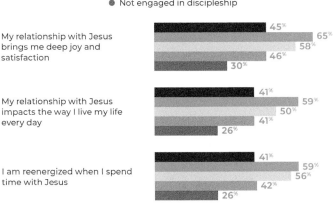

Walking with Jesus
% strongly agree

● All Christians ● In discipleship community
● Only discipling others ● Only being discipled
● Not engaged in discipleship

My relationship with Jesus brings me deep joy and satisfaction
- 45%
- 65%
- 58%
- 46%
- 30%

My relationship with Jesus impacts the way I live my life every day
- 41%
- 59%
- 50%
- 41%
- 26%

I am reenergized when I spend time with Jesus
- 41%
- 59%
- 56%
- 42%
- 26%

n=2,511 U.S. Christian adults, December 22, 2020–January 18, 2021.

The majority of all disciplemakers places high importance on their religious faith (71% of those in discipleship community, 65% of those only discipling others "strongly agree") and feels progress in their spiritual life is very important (68%, 46%). Further, they agree that one-on-one discipling relationships are crucial to that spiritual growth (59%, 45%). From another angle, more than half of those who see spiritual growth as very important (53%) are helping someone else grow in their faith (vs. 20% of those who don't think spiritual growth is "very important").

Time and again, an eagerness for discipleship coincides with an eagerness to grow in faith—and the inverse is also true. Christians who are not disciplemakers are less inclined to say their religious faith is very important in their life today (54% of those only being discipled, 40% of those not engaged in any

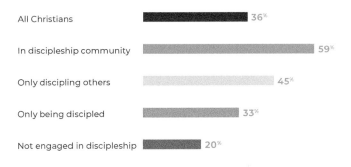

One-on-One Discipleship Relationships Are Seen as Important for Christians' Spiritual Growth

% say "very important"

All Christians	36%
In discipleship community	59%
Only discipling others	45%
Only being discipled	33%
Not engaged in discipleship	20%

n=2,511 U.S. Christian adults, December 22, 2020–January 18, 2021.

discipleship), to value seeing progress in their spiritual life (37%, 22% "very important") and to believe one-on-one relationships support spiritual growth (33%, 20%).

Do you value seeing progress in your spiritual life? Do you wish you would feel reenergized when you spend time with Jesus? If you want to grow spiritually in these kinds of ways, consider walking with others in discipleship.

Detours from Discipleship

Clearly, as we get to know those who prioritize discipleship community, we are meeting individuals who prioritize their spiritual life in general. To sincerely travel toward one means arriving at both.

But, as you might know, sometimes things get in the way.

When it comes to discipling others, not feeling qualified or equipped (37%) is the main barrier for Christians who aren't in this

EVERYDAY DISCIPLEMAKERS ON ... **THE JOYS OF WALKING TOGETHER**

" Seeing Christ change and impact a person's life gives me immense spiritual satisfaction. There is joy and growth when believers share their faith life-on-life."

" The benefits of discipleship are spiritual edification and growing as a church and in our personal relationships with Jesus. I think we benefit from hearing how God is working in each other's lives and hearing how the Holy Spirit speaks to each of us."

Reasons Christians Do Not Make Disciples

*Please select which item comes closest to describing why
you are not discipling another person currently.*

Don't think I am qualified / equipped — 37%

No one has suggested it / asked me — 24%

Just haven't thought about it — 22%

Had a bad experience in the past — 3%

Other — 14%

n=1,643 U.S. Christian adults who are not disciplemakers,
December 22, 2020–January 18, 2021.

66 It has become a true joy of my life to help people I care about—
extended family members, fellow soccer moms, neighbors and our
kids—invite the power and hope of Jesus into their lives. I've watched
the overflow of that hope turn into a vision to make disciples of Jesus
wherever the Lord takes them."

66 It keeps me focused on God's mission and Kingdom values. I am
constantly aware of my own walk. Knowing that I am investing in
someone else encourages me to invest in myself, so as not to lead
someone else astray. For others, I think it is really encouraging when
someone takes a genuine interest in them."

kind of relationship. This is true across all age groups. Additional Barna research shows that disinterest in disciplemaking is tied to a fear of not being good at it, of not having enough knowledge or of being the wrong person for the job. The confidence crisis is a core issue—and we'll devote the final section of *Growing Together* to exploring it. For now, know that if one of these reasons has held you back from helping others grow spiritually, you're not alone.

Whether because of this personal wariness around discipleship or more general indifference, some Christians who aren't making disciples seem only to need a push. One in four says the practice of discipling others hasn't been suggested to them (24%) or they haven't thought about helping someone grow closer to God (22%). Interestingly, a lack of external motivation becomes the chief obstacle for Christians who *are* being discipled themselves but *aren't* helping someone else grow in the same way; 31 percent (vs. 19% of Christians not engaged in any discipleship) say no one

EVERYDAY DISCIPLEMAKERS ON ... **THE JOYS OF WALKING TOGETHER**

❝ When I think about the research showing African Americans being so ready to be disciplemakers, my heart rejoices for my people! African Americans have learned how to persevere through adversity. They are people who know how to listen to the Spirit of God and to be led down pathways to advance the kingdom of God in creative ways. They are people who see family and community as a gateway to reach the next generation for Jesus and this is the heartbeat of discipleship."

Reasons Christians Are Not in a Discipleship Relationship

What are the reasons why you don't have a person like this in your life?
Select all that apply.

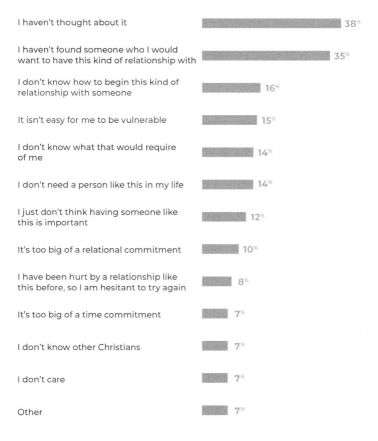

I haven't thought about it — 38%

I haven't found someone who I would want to have this kind of relationship with — 35%

I don't know how to begin this kind of relationship with someone — 16%

It isn't easy for me to be vulnerable — 15%

I don't know what that would require of me — 14%

I don't need a person like this in my life — 14%

I just don't think having someone like this is important — 12%

It's too big of a relational commitment — 10%

I have been hurt by a relationship like this before, so I am hesitant to try again — 8%

It's too big of a time commitment — 7%

I don't know other Christians — 7%

I don't care — 7%

Other — 7%

n=1,040 U.S. Christian adults not being discipled, December 22, 2020–January 18, 2021.

has suggested or asked that they disciple someone else, making this their top response. This implies encouragement to disciple others might be a key step to advance in this journey of growing together.

Similarly, when Christians don't have a relationship that provides accountability, support and spiritual growth, the main reason is that they either haven't thought about it (38%) or they haven't found someone with whom they want to have this type of relationship (35%). From these responses, we gather that invitations into spiritually fruitful relationships just aren't naturally occurring. What if you were asked? What if you were to ask someone else? You might assume busy schedules and an always-on culture would get in the way, but time (7%) or relational commitments (10%) are less likely to be reasons why discipleship relationships are not in place.

In summary, **lack of confidence, lack of thought and lack of opportunity are the greatest hurdles to discipleship,**

EVERYDAY DISCIPLEMAKERS ON … **BARRIERS TO DISCIPLESHIP**

" The primary barrier is consistent availability. Outside of the college environment, it has been challenging to develop relationships in which both parties can 'share life'—that is, engage together frequently enough to get to know each other as people and identify common interests as well as make time to study the Word together. This can be the result of physical distance (e.g., living / working far apart) or temporal distance (busyness or misaligned schedules). Ultimately, it reflects a lack of priority on intimate relationships, at least those outside of the nuclear family."

Christians tell Barna. Notably, the weight given to each reason varies across gender and generational lines. Although men are just as likely as women to be in a discipleship relationship, men who aren't in these relationships are more likely to say that they don't need a person like this in their life, that having someone like this is not important, that it's too big of a relational or time commitment, that they don't care, and that they don't know what would be required of them. On the other hand, one barrier stands out among women who aren't in discipleship relationships: They are more likely than their male peers to say they've been hurt by a relationship like this before. Hurdles to being discipled can be of a logistical, spiritual or emotional nature, depending on the experiences that have shaped us—in this case, navigating the world and the Church as a man or woman.

Older Christian generations, especially Boomers (43%), are more likely to say they haven't thought about discipleship

" I think it can be difficult to commit and find other people to commit to meeting consistently."

" People are very busy. Discipleship is competing with a lot of other things seeking people's time and attention."

" I don't hear discipleship talked about more than one to two times a year. What I hear talked about more is our discipleship under Jesus, that we are individually being discipled by him. There's little about community-based discipleship or one-on-one discipleship."

relationships (compared to 37% of Gen X, 29% of Millennials and Gen Z), while Millennials (21%) are more likely to say they don't know how to begin this type of relationship (compared to 15% of Gen X and 13% of Boomers).

Let's pause on this point: While Millennials struggle to get these relationships started and to find someone they want to connect with on this spiritual level, they are also the age group most likely to find one-on-one discipleship relationships important (44% vs. 33% Gen Z, 35% Gen X, 30% Boomers). In other words, their lack of engagement is not necessarily reflective of a lack of interest or even a lack of time. Many young adults care quite a bit about shared spiritual growth. But *caring* about discipleship is not the same as *participating* in it. ●

A Summary of Key Stats:

Over half of Christians (56%) say they have a relationship where they share accountability, support and spiritual growth with someone else.

One in three Christians (33%) says they currently and actively help someone to grow in their faith and move closer to Christ.

Discipleship correlates with feeling joyful and re-energized in one's relationship with Jesus.

Questions for Reflection:

Where do you fall in the spectrum of discipleship—are you investing in someone else? Being invested in? Both? Neither?

How much do you desire to grow closer to and more like Christ? What are you doing to move toward this goal?

Refer to the charts on pages 27 and 29. Is there something in your life that keeps you from either being discipled or making disciples? Which of those barriers would you say is most often *your* reason for not being in a discipleship relationship?

Questions to Ask Your Friends:

Do you see our relationship as one that offers accountability? Support? Encouragement? If not, how can we provide that to each other more often?

Do you think of relationships like ours as an element of your spiritual life or spiritual growth?

How does your relationship with Jesus or the time you spend with him make you feel?

Friends for the Road

**To find the purpose for disciplemaking,
look outside yourself**

Privacy might seem like the natural habitat for faith formation in our increasingly individualized culture.

Indeed, 56 percent of Christians feel their spiritual life is entirely private. This majority of Christians is less likely to say it is very important to see progress in their spiritual life (30% say progress is important vs. 54% of those who don't consider their faith private), less likely to say their faith is very important in their life today (45% vs. 66% agree strongly) and less likely to have weekly time with God (51% vs. 66%). In other words, the idea that faith should be kept private is one part of a bigger swirl of negative conditions that need to be addressed for people to see spiritual growth.

A private approach to spirituality is pervasive, even among Christians who *are* in discipleship community: 46 percent still say they consider their spiritual lives to be private, and that percentage climbs for younger Christians who are making disciples.

There is an interesting generational difference to note between older and younger Christians. Boomers are the generation least likely to be part of discipleship community and are also the generation most likely to believe their spiritual life is entirely private (63%). Gen Z, meanwhile, are more than twice as likely as Boomers to be part of discipleship community and are the least likely generation to believe their spiritual life is private (46%). At first glance, this data suggests a discipleship gap for Boomer Christians today.

Yet, the script flips among Boomers who say they are discipling others. These older adults *rarely* consider their spiritual lives to be private (23%). Among Christians discipling others, they actually become (by far!) the generation least likely to relegate spirituality to the private realm.

EVERYDAY DISCIPLEMAKERS ON ... **FINDING MOTIVATION TO SHARE**

What prompts Boomers to push past their generation's inclination toward privacy? These quotes from Boomer disciplemakers offer insight.

❝ We were created to be in community. Faith is not and cannot be a private matter."

❝ My goal is to have a positive impact on the lives of others as the lives of others have had a positive impact on me."

Boomer Disciplemakers Resist the Tendency to Treat Spirituality as Private

% say yes, their personal spiritual life is entirely private

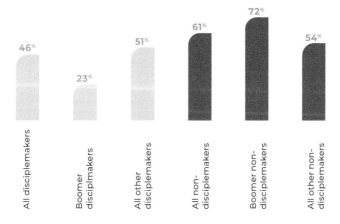

n=2,511 U.S. Christian adults, December 22, 2020–January 18, 2021.

" Jesus is the answer to so many personal issues that our communities face today. We cannot have peace in our communities and cities without God's grace being manifested in the lives of believers."

" Honestly, my heart goes out to people as I see them struggle and their hurts, wounds, fears, doubts and needs. I know how God has worked in my life in those areas and how good he and his outcomes are. The more I know and experience God, the more motivated I am to share him and how to go deep with him."

This speaks to a different mindset among the minority of Boomers who are discipling others—one we can all learn from. They have grasped a principle that contends with both their generational tendency toward isolation and a cultural tendency toward a largely interior spiritual life:

Ultimately, discipleship is not just about you.

Spirituality Loves Company

Even before the COVID-19 pandemic hit, individuals expressed feeling distant from others, and Christians are not exempt. Part of this can reasonably be attributed to the rhythms of our digital society. We have become accustomed to experiencing hyperconnection and disconnection all at once. Consider that, in a global study of 18–35-year-olds, Barna found that most young adults say events around the world matter to them (77%) and they feel connected to people around the world (57%)—even as only one

EVERYDAY DISCIPLEMAKERS ON … **SEEING FRIENDS GROW**

❝ Jesus has radically transformed my life, and I want others to experience that same gift. I want others to find freedom and healing like I have in Jesus."

❝ Both I and those I have discipled have come to a greater realization of our calling and responsibility to those around us."

in three young adults feels deeply cared for by those around them (33%) or that someone believes in them (32%).

Discipleship is a powerful way to meet a communal need for vulnerability and companionship. "Because we loved you so much, we were delighted to share with you not only the gospel of God but our lives as well," Paul writes to the Church in Thessalonica (1 Thessalonians 2:7–8). Those who are part of discipleship community seem to share this delight. Discipleship provides meaningful, growth-oriented friendships, confronts loneliness and shows love and care for others. In short, a Christian has many reasons to expand their social-spiritual life.

Remember, as defined in this study, people who are in discipleship relationships have at least one connection marked by mutual accountability, encouragement, support and spiritual growth. Disciplemaking involves actively helping someone else grow closer to Christ. These are generous, intentional and intimate

" I don't want to keep the good news to myself. I don't want others to feel discouraged and alone. It encourages my own walk to be able to walk alongside another Christian and see them grow."

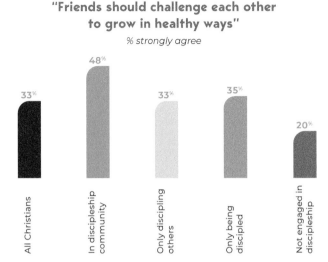

"Friends should challenge each other to grow in healthy ways"

% strongly agree

- All Christians: 33%
- In discipleship community: 48%
- Only discipling others: 33%
- Only being discipled: 35%
- Not engaged in discipleship: 20%

n=2,511 U.S. Christian adults, December 22, 2020–January 18, 2021.

connections! Thus, friendship is often foundational for healthy discipleship, and deeper friendship may also be one of the positive benefits that comes from a discipleship relationship.

Most Christians are aware of the need for this spiritual synergy. In fact, more than four out of five (82%) agree, one-third strongly so, that friends should challenge each other to grow in healthy ways. Unsurprisingly, almost half of Christians in discipleship community (48% vs. 20% of those not engaged in any discipleship) agree strongly with this idea.

Broken down by generation, about one-quarter of Boomers (23%), one-third of Gen X (33%) and about two in five Millennials (42%) and Gen Z (43%) strongly agree that friends should challenge each other to grow. Although younger Christian generations are more likely to believe that friendships should lead to healthy growth—and may be in a stage of life marked by more rich and more concentrated friendships to begin with—few in any age group disagree with this (at most, 21%, among Boomers).

Black Christians especially stand out in this conviction, with 45 percent expressing strong agreement that friendships should spark healthy growth (vs. 29% of white Christians, 36% Hispanic Christians).

The data suggest that, in general, American adults desire friendships that challenge them. That's vulnerable territory, but we've been given a strong role model.

When Jesus discipled the 12, the spiritual and day-to-day matters of their lives intermingled. Life was not private or compartmentalized. Meals and miracles, frustration and affection, sermons and naps, trials and celebrations—they shared it all. Christians should consider what it would mean to do the same today.

A Summary of Key Stats:

Most Christians feel their spiritual life is entirely private, though this belief softens among those engaged in making disciples.

Globally, young adults are more likely to feel connected to people around the world (57%) than to feel deeply cared for by those around them (33%).

More than four out of five Christians (82%) agree, one-third strongly so, that friends should challenge each other to grow in healthy ways.

Questions for Reflection:

Do you consider your spiritual life to be entirely or even just mostly private? Why or why not?

Do you struggle with feelings of isolation, loneliness or disconnection? If so, what aggravates those feelings? What calms them?

Past or present, how many of your friendships have challenged you to grow? In how many of your friendships have you challenged others to grow?

Questions to Ask Your Friends:

Do you feel drawn closer to God when you are with other people? How does that feel similar to or different from when you are drawn closer to God in moments by yourself?

Do you feel comfortable sharing spiritual things with me in this relationship? Why or why not?

Can you think of a time I have challenged you to change your mind or helped you to grow in some way?

The Disciple Cycle

**Being a disciple leads to making disciples leads
to being a more committed disciple**

When you learn to disciple others, you keep learning about how to
be a disciple yourself, and vice versa. As we navigate this *Growing
Together* journey arm-in-arm, it's helpful to consider what could be
called the "disciple cycle."

We see this cycle among Christians who are in discipleship
relationships or community. As the following charts show, those
who are in mutual discipleship relationships also place more value
and intention on following Jesus and practicing spiritual disciplines in their own lives. Disciplemaking correlates with these spiritual postures. Engagement with scripture, too, is strongly tied to
the entire discipleship cycle, both offering and receiving help for
spiritual growth.

Spiritual Growth Perspectives & Passions

% strongly agree

● All Christians ● In discipleship community
● Only discipling others ● Only being discipled
● Not engaged in discipleship

I want to see God's plan for my life more clearly

46%
58%
57%
49%
33%

I am passionate about loving Jesus deeply and fully

41%
63%
54%
40%
25%

I am passionate about becoming more and more like Jesus
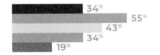
34%
55%
43%
34%
19%

I depend on the Holy Spirit to lead me
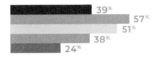
39%
57%
51%
38%
24%

I am purposeful to nurture and deepen my intimacy with Jesus
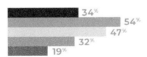
34%
54%
47%
32%
19%

n=2,511 U.S. Christian adults, December 22, 2020–January 18, 2021.

Frequency of Spiritual Practices

● All Christians   ● In discipleship community
○ Only discipling others   ● Only being discipled
● Not engaged in discipleship

Spend uninterrupted time alone with God at least once a week (reading the Bible, praying, worshipping or other Christian spiritual practices)

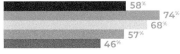

58%
74%
68%
57%
46%

Have time to regularly read the Bible

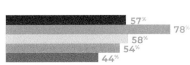

57%
78%
58%
54%
44%

Read the Bible in the past week

38%
71%
51%
31%
16%

Memorized a Bible verse in the past two months

27%
58%
35%
21%
7%

Distraction & Discipleship

I often get distracted when trying to spend time with God

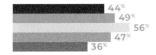

44%
49%
56%
47%
36%

n=2,511 U.S. Christian adults, December 22, 2020–January 18, 2021.

Disciplemakers' focus does not come without friction. Christians who are in discipleship relationships, in either direction, are like the average Christian when it comes to feeling distracted during their time with God. So be encouraged if you battle distraction during times of prayer, meditation or Bible study— you're not alone! Purposeful, motivated disciples push through this same feeling.

Following Directions

Jesus, the Apostle Paul and others encourage Christians to pursue a practice and a legacy of making disciples wherever they go.

- And you should imitate me, just as I imitate Christ.
  1 Corinthians 11:1
- So we tell others about Christ, warning everyone and teaching everyone with all the wisdom God has given us. We want

EVERYDAY DISCIPLEMAKERS ON ... **SPIRITUAL DISCIPLINES**

" Discipleship nurtured me in spiritual disciplines like spending time with Jesus, prayer, Bible study and memorizing scripture. It helped me develop concern for those far from Jesus and equipped me with skills to share my faith and help others grow."

" I have developed spiritual disciplines to strengthen and develop my relationship with God and have been challenged to encourage others to do the same."

to present them to God, perfect in their relationship to Christ. Colossians 1:28

- You have heard me teach things that have been confirmed by many reliable witnesses. Now teach these truths to other trustworthy people who will be able to pass them on to others. 2 Timothy 2:2

By this standard, **discipleship is meant to be core to the life of faith. It's not just for experts with degrees or years of experience.**

If you're honest with yourself, do you think it is *your responsibility* to help others grow spiritually? The research shows that only 27 percent of Christians strongly agree all Christians have a responsibility to spiritually invest in others. Another 44 percent somewhat agree. That's not a dismissal of the call to disciple others, but it's not exactly a pep rally for it either. Even Christians

" I began to closely study the life of Jesus and I observed that Jesus ministered to a lot of people, but he prayerfully chose and poured his life into a few (the 12 disciples) and commissioned them to do the same."

" Discipleship opened me to many things. First, I had someone consistent in my life that was willing to love me unconditionally. That meant the world to me and made me want to do the same for others. ... The person walked alongside me as I tried various practices (silence and solitude, evangelism, prayer, scripture memory, etc.) for the first time. Having me try all these practices helped me find a safe place to discover how I commune with God uniquely and intimately."

who aren't engaged in any form of discipleship muster this moderate level of agreement (13% strongly, 43% somewhat).

Those who are engaged in discipleship relationships seem to take this responsibility more personally. Forty-four percent of those in discipleship community and about three in 10 of those who are either being discipled (27%) or discipling others (31%) strongly agree Christians are expected to spiritually invest in others.

At the end of the day—and here, at the end of this section— it's worth remembering what discipleship and disciplemaking ultimately are: a calling and a mandate. Yes, they can feel inspiring and rewarding. Yes, they fill social gaps in your life and in the lives of

Multiplying Disciples

The Great Commission is an ongoing call to go and make disciples. Thus, continued multiplication or "paying it forward" is an essential mark of discipleship.

For most, however, moving from insular faith to interpersonal growth is a big, transformative leap on its own. Motivating friends to then go and do the same for others may seem like too much to hope for. The majority of Christians (70%) considers a discipleship relationship successful even if it stops at shared personal growth in following Jesus without ever feeling inspired or equipped to mentor others in the same way.

Interestingly, Christians who are making disciples are even *more* likely to feel replication isn't a necessary outcome of discipleship (32% strongly agree). Their own experiences are roughly split: Just over half of all Christians who are discipling others (55%, including 60% of those in discipleship community) say that, to their knowledge, the person they are helping is in turn helping others grow closer to Christ.

"I think all Christians have a responsibility to spiritually invest in others"

% strongly agree

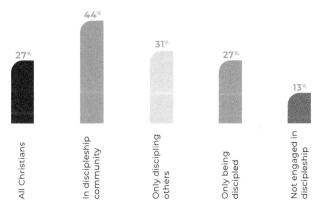

n=2,511 U.S. Christian adults, December 22, 2020–January 18, 2021.

those you love. Yes, they channel the widespread desire to become a more spiritually mature Christian. But before and beneath all that, they are the substance of one of Jesus' strongest commands, delivered with the weight of his full authority "in heaven and on earth," in some of his final words to his followers (Matthew 28: 19–20).

Even if you come to discipleship community by way of some other personal desire or social opportunity, that journey will still reveal, through growing closer to God, that to follow him is to be sent out (Matthew 4:19).

Anyone and everyone who walks with Jesus is included in the scriptural, relational calling to make disciples—including you.

Together, we've learned how being a disciple and making disciples can meet some of your spiritual and social needs. Further, they position you to bring God's hope into the lives of your friends. He has put you in their lives and them in yours for a reason.

What if, together, you can grow even closer to him?

EVERYDAY DISCIPLEMAKERS ON ... **THE URGENCY OF DISCIPLESHIP**

❝ This is not just the responsibility of spiritual leaders. Every believer should be equipped to impact where they work, live and worship."

❝ The game-changer for me was when a dear brother in Christ challenged me by saying that the Great Commission was not just for the 12 disciples but was for me as well! This life-changing exhortation put me on a pilgrimage to become like Jesus in his character and to embrace his mission for me and all of us who claim him as our king."

A Summary of Key Stats:

Christians who are engaged in discipleship regularly spend time with God and in his word—even if they are still inclined to get distracted.

Only 27 percent of Christians strongly agree all Christians have a responsibility to spiritually invest in others.

The majority of Christians (70%) considers a discipleship relationship successful even if it does not lead to inspiring or equipping individuals to mentor others in the same way.

" How could I not share about my spiritual life? It is the core of real life. The scripture calls us to a whole-life discipleship, from Genesis to Revelation."

" God has revealed to me his character and his faithfulness in many ways, one way being the witness of other people who have discipled me. I want to encourage others in their walk with Jesus and witness to how God transforms us (and me)."

Questions for Reflection:

Are you purposeful about your spiritual disciplines? Do other people in your life help fuel those passions or practices?

How often does a time of prayer or scripture study compel you toward meaningful experiences or conversations with others?

Do you consider it a calling and responsibility to spiritually invest in others? Do the people who spiritually mentor you inspire you to mentor others in turn?

Questions to Ask Your Friends:

What does uninterrupted time with God look like for you? Do you structure or nurture that time in specific ways?

Could you tell me about a verse that has stood out to you, maybe even one you memorized?

How would you describe the feeling of being led by the Holy Spirit in moments in your own life?

PART 2:

What Day-To-Day Discipleship Can Look Like

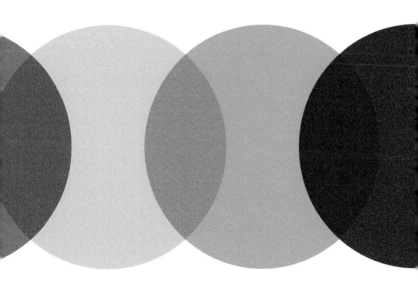

The Matter of Time

You aren't too busy to be in discipleship community

Interest in a lifestyle of discipleship is not in short supply. In a 2020 study, we discovered that 67 percent of U.S. Christians are interested in intentionally helping people learn from and live more like Jesus by praying with them, studying the Bible together and sharing in experiences of everyday life (28% definitely interested, 39% somewhat interested).

Clearly, many Christians—including you, we're assuming— want discipleship to be a part of their day-to-day lives. The first section of *Growing Together* explored some of the spiritual and social benefits reported by those who already experience growth in community. We know that discipleship beckons us toward a more bountiful relationship with God and with others. In many ways, discipleship is the fruit of a "tree planted by the water, that sends out its roots by the stream ... its leaves remain green ... it does not cease to bear fruit" (Jeremiah 17:8).

Still, our research for *Growing Together* has established the fact that 44 percent of all Christians are not being discipled through a relationship in which they share accountability, support and spiritual growth. And just one-third of Christians (33%) is categorized by Barna as a disciplemaker, actively helping someone grow in faith and move closer to Christ. Overall, that leaves about two in five Christians lacking any kind of discipleship community.

If the desire is so strong, the calling is so clear and the benefits are so plain, what is holding back Christians from discipleship?

Is there anything holding *you* back?

This section seeks to address practical and relational hurdles and help Christians realize what day-to-day discipleship can look like.

Put Discipleship on the Schedule

We lead busy, distracted lives. Amid work, social functions, school, church, keeping up with all that's going on in the world and still holding onto the dream of free time, the thought of adding another item to an already packed schedule may feel overwhelming. Lack of time and competing daily priorities seem like obvious obstacles to developing discipleship community.

That is, they *seem* like obstacles. Are these barriers actually that high?

Indeed, even Barna researchers were surprised to learn that our hyper-productive, constantly connected, over-scheduled culture may not be the *primary* reason discipleship doesn't occur.

Reasons Christians Are Not in a Discipleship Relationship

What are the reasons why you don't have a person like this in your life?
Select all that apply.

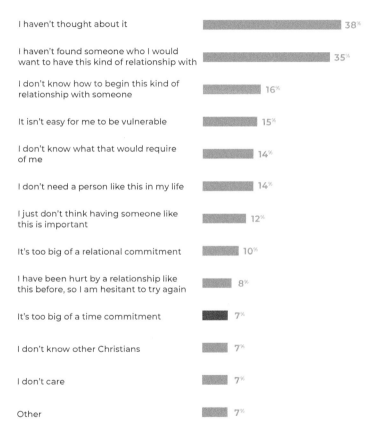

I haven't thought about it	38%
I haven't found someone who I would want to have this kind of relationship with	35%
I don't know how to begin this kind of relationship with someone	16%
It isn't easy for me to be vulnerable	15%
I don't know what that would require of me	14%
I don't need a person like this in my life	14%
I just don't think having someone like this is important	12%
It's too big of a relational commitment	10%
I have been hurt by a relationship like this before, so I am hesitant to try again	8%
It's too big of a time commitment	7%
I don't know other Christians	7%
I don't care	7%
Other	7%

n=1,040 U.S. Christian adults not being discipled,
December 22, 2020–January 18, 2021.

As the highlighted bar in the chart shows, few Christians who aren't being discipled say the time commitment (7%) is a reason they don't have someone who disciples them. Fourteen percent are deterred by a vague understanding of discipleship, saying they just don't know what such a relationship would require of them. But overall, insecurities, lack of intention or absence of close friendships emerge as greater perceived challenges.

We also learned in the previous section that followers of Christ manage to find moments for their own private spiritual disciplines. This might look like having uninterrupted time with God each week or regularly reading the Bible, practices reported by the majority of Christians—especially those who also experience discipleship relationships and community.

Of course, people still view their time as something valuable to steward or, if needed, scrounge. For example, Barna's research shows that people are still looking for time-savers, such as brief

EVERYDAY DISCIPLEMAKERS ON … CREATING TIME FOR DISCIPLESHIP

❝ Time management is the greatest challenge. Praying with and for others is a great way to incorporate discipleship."

❝ Orienting myself around the Word each day helps me maintain a Kingdom perspective and keeps scripture fresh in my mind so that it is more accessible to me when opportunities arise during conversations with others."

Challenges to Becoming a Disciplemaker

Base: Christians who are very or somewhat interested in disciplemaking

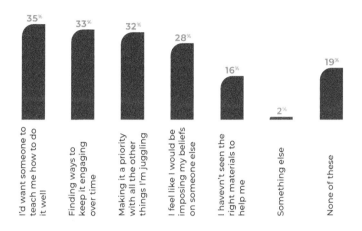

35%	I'd want someone to teach me how to do it well
33%	Finding ways to keep it engaging over time
32%	Making it a priority with all the other things I'm juggling
28%	I feel like I would be imposing my beliefs on someone else
16%	I havevn't seen the right materials to help me
2%	Something else
19%	None of these

n=1,536 U.S. Christian adults, June 1–July 4, 2020.

" I like to wake up and get in 30 minutes with God (if possible) before getting into my day. Sometimes that's sitting in silence, sometimes it's reading poetry, sometimes it's listening to a *lectio divina* meditation on Hallow, and sometimes it's reading the Bible. Usually, God gives me something to think about for the rest of the day from that time."

" I spend significant time in the Word, especially as it relates to the topic on my heart or need of the moment, and working with God as to what obedience in that area, in a specific detail of my life, looks like."

Bible studies or quick lessons, when it comes to learning about discipleship. After all, roughly half of Christians, even those engaged in discipleship, admit to often getting distracted during time with God.

Further, people want time investments in discipleship to feel like a meaningful addition. One in three Christians who has interest in disciplemaking worries about how to keep things engaging for the long haul (33%) or how to set disciplemaking as a priority, considering all the other things they are juggling (32%). Some groups especially wrestle with how to add discipleship to their to-do lists—for instance, non-white Christians (48% vs. 30% white Christians), Christians who have young children (36% vs. 29% without children) and those with full-time jobs (37% vs. 30% part-time employed, 26% unemployed).

Still, such concerns aren't guaranteed to be barriers.

EVERYDAY DISCIPLEMAKERS ON … **CREATING TIME FOR DISCIPLESHIP**

" You can incorporate discipleship into daily life by spreading Bible studies out over several days, doing 15–30 minutes at a sitting and proactively scheduling time with believers and unbelievers on a regular basis."

" You need to be intentional about making time to disciple others. Share good online resources and tools that will encourage people to grow and be accountable."

"I struggle to find time for community with other Christians since my pace of life is so busy"

● Agree strongly ● Agree somewhat
● Disagree somewhat ● Disagree strongly

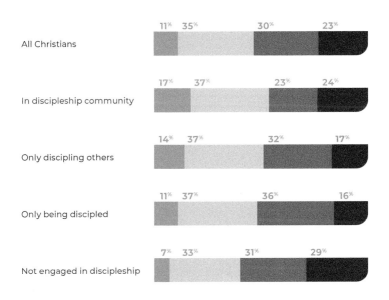

All Christians — 11% 35% 30% 23%

In discipleship community — 17% 37% 23% 24%

Only discipling others — 14% 37% 32% 17%

Only being discipled — 11% 37% 36% 16%

Not engaged in discipleship — 7% 33% 31% 29%

n=2,511 U.S. Christian adults, December 22, 2020–January 18, 2021.

Consider this: Who do you think are some of the people most likely to struggle with finding time for Christian community because their pace of life is so busy?

The answer: Christians who are *already in* discipleship community—those both receiving and giving discipleship in their relationships. They are actively prioritizing this spiritual exchange

All in a Day's Discipleship

How do Christians think about stewarding their time toward spiritual growth?

TIME WITH OTHERS

NEARLY HALF of Christians struggle to find time for community with other Christians because they are too busy

TWO IN FIVE Christians agree it is difficult to figure out how to balance spending time with their church community and with non-Christians

ONE IN THREE Christians is very willing to invest time in others to pass along what they have learned in life

TIME WITH GOD

of Christians spend uninterrupted time with God at least weekly

44% of Christians often get distracted when trying to spend time with God

57% of Christians have time to regularly read the Bible

41% of Christians strongly agree they are reenergized when they spend time with Jesus

TIME TO COMMIT

JUST 7% of Christians who aren't yet in a discipleship relationship attribute this to the time commitment

ONE IN THREE Christians who are interested in disciplemaking assumes it will be a challenge to prioritize it alongside all the things they are juggling

62% of Christians who are uninterested in disciplemaking say it sounds like too big of a time commitment

of potential disciplemakers who don't have the right materials say they want brief Bible studies

ONE IN FOUR potential disciplemakers, if they could build their own discipleship resource, favors quick lessons

n=2,511 U.S. Christian adults, December 22, 2020–January 18, 2021.
n=1,536 U.S. Christian adults, June 1–July 4, 2020.

in their busy schedules, which isn't easy but, as the research has shown us, produces deep rewards. Thus, these disciples and disciplemakers are more likely than other Christians to know the struggle of prioritizing spiritual growth and friendship in their fast-paced lives—yet it doesn't stop them.

This is a key lesson in realizing the calling of day-to-day discipleship: Those who experience discipleship community have the time or will make the time. Or perhaps even reimagine or divvy up that time! Barna's findings suggest the decisive factor is not who has the hours in the day, but who is willing to creatively commit from the hours they do have to growing in their faith and becoming qualified or equipped to help others grow, too.

A Summary of Key Stats:

Two-thirds of U.S. Christians are at least somewhat interested in disciplemaking. Yet only one-third is actively helping someone else to grow closer to God.

Worries about time commitments are not identified as primary barriers to discipleship; they rank below insecurities, lack of intention or absence of close friendships as perceived challenges.

About half of Christians feel it's a struggle to make time in their busy schedule for Christian community. Christians who are in discipleship relationships acknowledge they share this struggle, but they work through it and report rich benefits.

Questions for Reflection:

What life priorities—even ones that require regular effort or feel like a "time crunch"—do you manage to make room for in your schedule? How do you do this?

Is it a struggle for you to find the time or energy to cultivate intentional, accountable relationships with other Christians? What other logistical, practical hurdles get in the way of your discipleship and disciplemaking?

What does intentional, uninterrupted time with God need to look like for you? What disciplines and decisions does it require of you to make sure it happens?

Questions to Ask Your Friends:

What do you always make time for in your schedule and routine? When does spiritual growth get accounted for?

How can we prioritize time together to pray, study the Bible or talk about our faith journeys and questions? Can we get something on the calendar, choose a plan or set a reminder?

How can I be respectful of your time and help you steward it well?

Relationship Routines

**Regular connections and everyday spaces
can cultivate spiritual growth**

Even more than worrying about not having enough time to participate in discipleship community, Christians fret about another finite resource: their energy—specifically, their energy for spiritually significant relationships and interactions that they assume will require a lot from them.

Have you felt this way? You're in good company. And you may also be getting in your own way by putting too much pressure on yourself or these friendships. Let's return to one of the charts we've seen before with a different filter.

Note how relational absences or concerns surface prominently (and throughout) the list of reasons Christians aren't participating in discipleship. Whether they need to invest in meeting new people, identify the right mentor or grow their capacity for

Social Reasons Christians Are
Not in a Discipleship Relationship

What are the reasons why you don't have a person like this in your life?
Select all that apply.

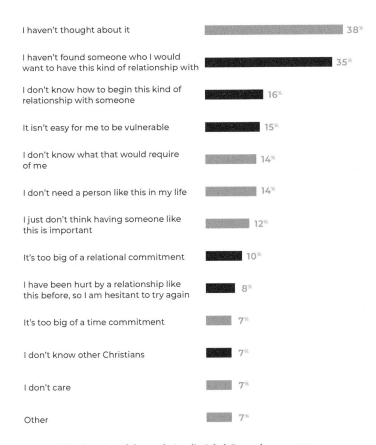

I haven't thought about it	38%
I haven't found someone who I would want to have this kind of relationship with	35%
I don't know how to begin this kind of relationship with someone	16%
It isn't easy for me to be vulnerable	15%
I don't know what that would require of me	14%
I don't need a person like this in my life	14%
I just don't think having someone like this is important	12%
It's too big of a relational commitment	10%
I have been hurt by a relationship like this before, so I am hesitant to try again	8%
It's too big of a time commitment	7%
I don't know other Christians	7%
I don't care	7%
Other	7%

n=1,040 U.S. Christian adults not being discipled, December 22, 2020–January 18, 2021.

vulnerability, many Christians perceive that discipleship will add some effort to their routines.

Christians with interest in disciplemaking also believe they will first need someone to teach them how to disciple others well; 35 percent in this group expect this will be a challenge to helping others follow Christ. It may be daunting to think about needing a coaching relationship just to get into other discipleship relationships!

We'll return to issues of gaining confidence and embracing vulnerability soon enough. These are the chief obstacles to experiencing the fullness of discipleship relationships, and thus the focus of the third and final section. For now, we'll continue to focus on overcoming some of the more logistical, day-to-day hurdles—in this case, gaps in social circles.

Meeting the Demand for Discipleship

It's striking that more than one-third of Christians who don't have a relationship that promotes accountability and spiritual growth (35%) is paralyzed simply by not having found someone to have this kind of relationship with. Given that we know two-thirds of U.S. Christians are interested in relationships like these, who are these individuals missing? Who is missing them?

It seems one solution lies in finding more intersections and better connections with each other, allowing Christians to put their desire for spiritual community and growth into practice. Where might these introductions occur?

The local church remains a natural and healthy hub for discipleship community. By far, when Christians have a group of peers who invest in one another and help each other grow closer to God, they tend to meet at church (56%). Beyond this common ground, family members (33%) and mutual friends (25%) foster discipleship connections. Other Christians team up with fellow disciples at work (18%), through a Christian group outside their church (17%) or even through relationships from childhood (21%). The list goes on, and the following visualization shows discipleship community's reach through schools, the internet and hobbies.

Clearly, **Christians shouldn't limit the places and spaces where they might find relationships** that could be compatible for discipleship. Whether stemming from a new encounter or re-investment in an existing connection, discipleship arises in many spheres of life.

Christians should also consider that, by prioritizing time and routines that allow for discipleship community, they may not be adding a relational burden but instead finding allies to share their other burdens. For the most part, Christians say they would feel

EVERYDAY DISCIPLEMAKERS ON ... **MAKING CONNECTIONS DAY-TO-DAY**

" If your routine brings you into contact or fellowship with certain people, go with it, instead of having to seek people out near and far. Meet people where they're at—some may just want to chat, others may be willing to open up, others may be willing to sit down with you for a Bible study."

" I have found that it is sometimes easier for people to have conversations about their spiritual lives when walking side-by-side. I mean that literally: I often initiate connection by inviting someone to take a walk."

How Christians Meet Their Discipleship Community

11% AT SCHOOL

11% THROUGH CHARITY WORK / VOLUNTEERISM EFFORTS

11% THROUGH MY HOBBIES

25% THROUGH MUTUAL FRIENDS

21% FROM CHILDHOOD

56% AT CHURCH

33% FAMILY MEMBERS

13% NEIGHBORS

12% ONLINE

18% AT WORK

17% THROUGH A CHRISTIAN COMMUNITY / GROUP OUTSIDE OF CHURCH

n=1,409 U.S. Christian adults with a group of Christians in their life who help them grow, December 22–January 18, 2021.

" To become familiar to others, you have to be consistently present where they are. Finding ways to be a part of some form of community, other than work or a church service, on a regular basis can help create room for discipleship relationships to form."

" Small group is where I'm able to give and receive encouragement and wisdom from other Christians who I trust."

comfortable walking through periods of hardship or suffering with others (36% very comfortable, 45% somewhat comfortable). For those who are in discipleship community—both offering and receiving spiritual mentorship—that percentage grows, suggesting **the comfort level with processing the raw, tough parts of friendship increases in a discipleship relationship.**

At the end of the day, as Christians contemplate introducing themselves to someone new, inviting someone to coffee or a Bible study, broaching a spiritual discussion with a friend or straight-up asking a mentor to enter a relationship of accountability and spiritual encouragement with them, they may find an eager party on the other end. At the moment, just one in five U.S. adults (22%) says their friends care about and contribute to their personal growth. With a bit of boldness, openness and intentionality, even in existing friendships, that number might be boosted considerably.

EVERYDAY DISCIPLEMAKERS ON ... **MAKING CONNECTIONS DAY-TO-DAY**

❝ My discipleship process involves several people along the years. It was not one person, but many thoughtful Bible studies, observations and conversations. Those relationships were formed in my neighborhood, workplace, community and church by networks of relationships."

Disciples Walk Through Hard Times with Friends

*As a friend, how comfortable are you with helping people
through periods of suffering (mourning, hardship, etc.)?*

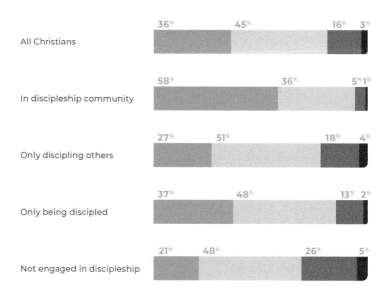

● Very comfortable   ○ Somewhat comfortable
● Not very comfortable   ● Not at all comfortable

	Very comfortable	Somewhat comfortable	Not very comfortable	Not at all comfortable
All Christians	36%	45%	16%	3%
In discipleship community	58%	36%	5%	1%
Only discipling others	27%	51%	18%	4%
Only being discipled	37%	48%	13%	2%
Not engaged in discipleship	21%	48%	26%	5%

n=2,511 U.S. Christian adults, December 22, 2020–January 18, 2021.

A Summary of Key Stats:

Only 22 percent of U.S. adults strongly agree their friends care about and contribute to their personal growth.

Thirty-five percent of Christians who don't have a relationship that promotes accountability and spiritual growth say they have not found someone to have this kind of relationship with.

Church is the primary place that Christians meet groups of people who invest in shared spiritual growth. Family, friends, work and other spheres of life also offer opportunities to connect with people who might be interested in exploring or following Jesus together.

Questions for Reflection:

Is there untapped potential in your current social circle for more meaningful discussions, accountability and shared spiritual development?

Are there hobbies or realms of life where you could be more engaged and open to people?

Knowing that many Christians want deeper relationships but are waiting for a connection or suggestion, can you think of someone you'd like to invite into intentional and shared spiritual growth? Who? What will you do about this?

Questions to Ask Your Friends:

Do you have friends you trust? With whom you can share confessions and convictions? With whom you could process suffering and hardship?

What areas of your life feel rich in connections or friendships? Can you tell me more about what makes these relationships special?

What keeps you from meeting new people or feeling close to people you know? On the other hand, what helps you feel comfortable, open, inspired and supported?

Find Your Next Step

Practical, spiritual and relational tips to help you prioritize discipleship through various stages of life

Thus far, we've looked at some of the perceived daily challenges to discipleship and how we can practically organize our lives so that they become fertile ground for spiritual growth. Your discipleship journey is your own, and no single survey, chapter or book can provide a formula for meaningful discipleship community in your routine—your household, your office hours, your free time, your friend groups or your quiet moments with God.

Even so, looking at demographic trends across Barna's study, the numbers lead us to some recommendations that begin to add-ress the everyday realities of specific groups of Christians. Here, we'll look at some of the patterns among men and women, married and single Christians, parents and non-parents and older and younger disciples.

We'll examine their perceptions and habits from a few angles: their personal spiritual disciplines, their relational successes and hang-ups, as well as their potential for faith-sharing with people who are new to or outside the faith.

As you read, look for your own experiences, but also for descriptions of others in your life or network. Where are you motivated? Where can you lean in? Where can you reach out? Where is God drawing you closer to him and to others?

In the third section, Why You're More Ready Than You Think for Disciplemaking, we'll go even deeper into questions around vulnerability and security and what it means to boldly step into discipleship community.

To experience day-to-day discipleship ...

Christian men may need to:

LEARN THE VALUE OF DISCIPLESHIP RELATIONSHIPS

Christian men are more likely than women to worry about the relational commitment of being discipled. They are more likely to believe they don't even need a person in their life to share mutual accountability, support and spiritual growth, and to feel such relationships aren't important. This tracks with the fact that Christian men are less likely than Christian women to believe all Christians have a responsibility to disciple others.

Closer study of scripture and the life of Christ certainly underscores discipleship as an essential aspect of spiritual growth, which might require a new kind of humility and intimacy from some men. For others, the value of discipleship may become apparent when they've found the right group or experienced the transformative potential of discipleship community firsthand—which is likely to start by connecting with others in a congregation.

Almost 60 percent of men who have a group of trusted friends who help them grow closer to Jesus say they've found these relationships through church. Of course, some men find these circles in other environments, too. For instance, 31 percent say they met this group of people through family members, and 27 percent say they met them through mutual friends. Men are also more likely than women to meet such people through work (20% vs. 16%).

INTEGRATE TIME WITH GOD INTO THEIR DAILY LIVES

We have already covered "the disciple cycle"—the idea that making disciples begins with being a disciple. In other words, you can't help others grow closer to someone you don't know.

About two in five Christian men strongly agree that their relationship with God impacts the way they live their life (38%) and say they depend on the Holy Spirit to lead them (36%)—notable proportions, yet they lag behind the percentages of women who say the same (43%, 41%). The data point to a need for men to develop deeper intimacy with Jesus. In general, men are less likely than women to report spending uninterrupted time with God. Only 24 percent say they are able to have this time with God every day, compared to one in three Christian women (32%).

Men who struggle to prioritize or feel motivated to integrate time with God into their daily lives may need to cultivate diligence and get creative. Reading the Bible, praying, worshipping, meditating and other spiritual practices are worth folding into routines and lead to greater intimacy with God and his people.

Christian women may need to:

BE MINDFUL OF DISTRACTIONS

Women are more likely than men to say they are often distracted when spending time with God; 47 percent of women agree with this statement, compared to 40 percent of men. Women who have children in the home are slightly more likely to admit to struggling with distractions (52% vs. 46%), but as almost half of women without children still express this sentiment, these distractions can't solely be chalked up to family responsibilities that women often shoulder.

Time with God will not always be distraction-free. However, finding ways to focus on Jesus deepens relationships with him and others—something Christians who are in discipleship community affirm.

EVERYDAY DISCIPLEMAKERS ON ... **THEIR DISCIPLESHIP ACTIVITIES**

" Primarily, my wife and I use recreation as a means of getting to know people. I lead a men's discipleship study via Zoom and a golf-based fellowship group at a public golf course. We play nine holes of golf, talking while we play, and then we sit and have a discussion afterwards for 30–60 minutes, picking a topic to interact over."

EXPAND THEIR CIRCLE

Research suggests some Christian women have a narrow set of re-lationships. For example, almost half (48%) say it is hard to let new people into their life, and a similar percentage (45%) say they don't have one genuine friendship with someone who does not know Jesus. Women are also slightly less likely than men to say they spend meaningful time with non-Christians. Christian women may need to make a concentrated effort to connect with new Christians or non-Christians.

As their spiritual and social circle expands, these women may have to remember that discipleship is not merely a one-time in-teraction but a practice of continually expanding the Kingdom of God. Jesus taught his disciples to make disciples, calling Christ-followers to produce Christ-followers who will go and do likewise, wherever they go. Yet less than half of Christian women who are discipling others (47%) say they know the person they're currently

" I'm teaching men to make disciples where they are. Whether it's on the job or in the hood, having a younger disciple travel with me when meeting with other disciples for accountability is important. I encourage the people I disciple to attend conferences with like-minded believers for encouragement. I try to discover Bible studies focused on discipling."

discipling is helping others move closer to Christ as well. For context, nearly two-thirds of their male peers (63%) say the replication of disciples is occurring.

ADDRESS HURT FROM PAST RELATIONSHIPS
It's important to note the reality that *many* women—too many—have experienced pain at the hands of people who should have supported them. Overall, nearly three-quarters of Christian women (73%) say they've been hurt by someone they deeply trusted, compared to 56 percent of Christian men. One in 10 women who aren't being discipled (11%) goes so far as to say past hurts make them hesitant to try entering spiritually accountable relationships again (vs. 6% of men who aren't being discipled).

Prayerful, careful healing from relational trauma, perhaps with guidance from experts and mentors, may be crucial for some women to feel comfortable developing close relationships.

EVERYDAY DISCIPLEMAKERS ON … **THEIR DISCIPLESHIP ACTIVITIES**

" I read the Word, pray, do Bible study with other adults and my own family. I pursue openness, honesty and vulnerability in Christ in my marriage. Because of how much joy it brings to my own life, I am encouraged to share that with others."

" I disciple many through my counseling practice, engage with men in my small group one-on-one outside our meetings and disciple my kids daily."

Whether this healing precedes discipleship community or is a by-product of it, healthy Christian friendships could be an antidote for many women who have experienced the opposite.

Married Christians may need to:

LOOK FOR DISCIPLESHIP RELATIONSHIPS BEYOND THE FAMILY UNIT

Married Christians may not recognize the importance of discipleship relationships outside of their home. They are less likely than Christians who have never been married (55% vs. 62%) to say they have a relationship with someone other than a family member who offers them accountability and encourages them to grow spiritually.

Meaningful, Christ-centered friendships with people in all stages of life can give married people perspectives that a spouse might not. They also offer external accountability and provide an opportunity to help someone else grow closer to God.

EVALUATE STANDARDS OF FRIENDSHIP

Only 29 percent of married Christians strongly agree that friends should challenge each other to grow in healthy ways. Similarly, only 29 percent say they have confessed and processed sin with a friend in the last year.

By comparison, single Christians are more likely to see these practices as necessary components of friendship; 37 percent strongly agree that friends should challenge each other to grow in healthy ways, and 37 percent have confessed and processed sin with a friend in the past year.

This isn't the first time Barna research has shown that married couples (especially those without kids) can become too comfortable, isolated or focused inward. It's important for them to welcome mentorship, hold strong expectations for time with friends and invite iron to sharpen iron (Proverbs 27:17).

Single Christians may need to:

OVERCOME A RELUCTANCE TO SHARE

Across Barna's studies, Christian singles often demonstrate a love of and openness with their community that other Christians can learn from. Yet some single adults feel uneasy expressing their thoughts about faith specifically.

For example, more than one-quarter of Christians who have never been married (26%) says they are not comfortable sharing what they learn from the Bible with others. Further, almost one in five singles who aren't in a discipleship relationship says they are held back by a struggle to be vulnerable.

Finding people and opportunities that further spiritual growth is a challenge for the single Christian to embrace. Not only that, singles may also have to learn to trust that their spiritual insights *matter* to others and strengthen the body of Christ. Practicing vulnerability can be nerve-wracking, but it helps faith and relationships grow.

Christian parents may need to:

GET OUT OF THEIR BUBBLES

Barna research has previously shown that communal and spiritual activity increases in households with children present. In this study, we see relational values—such as confessing sins, walking through suffering together or challenging one another to grow—are also boosted among parents. Yet Christian parents may still miss natural opportunities for disciplemaking *and* evangelism.

Many Christians with kids have chances to develop deeper relationships with non-Christians. They often report having genuine friendships with people who don't know Jesus (66% vs. 55% without kids in the home). Almost three in 10 Christian parents spend meaningful time with non-Christians at least once a week, perhaps reflecting how the activities and communities that accompany raising kids add organically to a family's schedule and social circle.

At the same time, Christian parents tend to agree that it is difficult for them to balance church relationships and non-Christian relationships (50% vs. 36% of Christian non-parents), they're afraid to have spiritual conversations with non-Christians (28% vs. 22%) and they struggle to relate to non-Christians (28% vs. 16%).

For Christians in seasons of growing their families and raising kids, pursuing holistic discipleship may mean breaking out of a "Christian bubble," practicing hospitality or developing comfort in introducing spiritual topics in conversation.

Younger generations may need to:

SEEK OUT CHRISTIAN MENTORS

Gen Z and Millennials are in relatively social seasons of life—pursuing education, building careers, choosing neighborhoods and starting families. Generationally, they place high value on friendships. These generations have a more diverse ethnic makeup and keep more diverse community compared to their elders.

These are commendable patterns in young adults' lives. However, it means some young Christians don't naturally come by other meaningful Christian connections, or at least ones that challenge their spiritual growth or drive them toward discipleship. For young adults who aren't in discipleship relationships, some of the top barriers include little awareness of this type of community or being unsure where to begin. Gen Z and Millennial Christians also assert that their pace of life keeps them from finding time for Christian friends, who they are less likely to have in the first place.

Beyond their churches, young Christians report meeting other disciples through work, school or even online. With the Christian friends they do make or have, young adults could choose to be that oft-missing catalyst: a friend willing to propose starting a discipleship relationship.

Finally, roughly one-third of Gen Z and Millennial Christians says they struggle to engage with people from other generations. Their interactions may need to be reframed as opportunities to welcome the wisdom of older spiritual mentors into their lives.

Older generations may need to:

CONTINUE TO LEAN INTO CHURCH AND FAITH ENGAGEMENT

Despite being the generation most likely to spend uninterrupted time with God each day, Boomers are the generation least likely to either read their Bible regularly or share what they learn from scripture.

Further, while the pandemic disrupted plenty of Christians' church routines, Boomers in Barna's research are consistently less engaged in the life of a congregation, whether through general attendance or specific groups and activities.

Time spent reading scripture or being involved with a local church is foundational to meeting and making disciples, and can enrich the spiritual lives of even the most "experienced" Christians.

PRACTICE BEING OPEN TO OTHERS

Across the generations from youngest to oldest, we see a decline in the percentage of Christians who practice confession with trusted friends or who feel comfortable processing suffering or hardship with others. It comes as no surprise, then, that the percentage who say their spiritual life is entirely private correspondingly climbs, peaking with nearly two-thirds of Boomer Christians (63%) who agree.

Additionally, older generations exhibit a level of indifference toward discipling others. Roughly one in four Gen X or Boomer Christians who aren't in such a relationship says they just haven't thought about it. Overall, they are less likely than their younger peers to experience discipleship in community or to say they even want such groups or relationships.

Older Christians may need to be reminded or urged to partner with others in faith—through the good and the bad, the breakthroughs and the mundane moments. They have much to share with members of the family of God, old and young alike, and much to gain from the joy and challenge of life-to-life relationships.

Being a disciple and making disciples aren't just idealistic callings that few Christians can attain. Discipleship community is available to all who are intentional in making room for it—in their schedules, in their social circles and in their hearts.

A Summary of Key Stats:

Christian men may need reminders of the value of discipleship relationships and the importance of time with God. Christian women could benefit from distraction-free space and seeking out broader, deeper connections.

Married Christians may need to seize opportunities to spiritually invest outside the home and embrace healthy challenges in friendships. Single Christians have room to grow their trust that they can share about their faith journey. Christians who are raising kids have varied and vibrant community which they could engage with more intentionally.

Younger Christians may need to seek out Christian friendships—even intergenerational ones that may seem awkward or fraught. Older Christians face a challenge to stay open and engaged in spiritual community and recognize the power of sharing from their faith story.

Questions for Reflection:

Where do you find yourself in this season of life? How did the trends in this chapter speak to you? Where were they not relevant or true of your experience?

Do some of these patterns from the research help you understand family members, peers or friends better?

To make discipleship and disciplemaking a goal, what is one practical change you're going to make in your day-to-day priorities or routines after reading this section?

Questions to Ask Your Friends:

Do you struggle to engage with people of other generations, backgrounds or stages of life? Why or why not?

Does it help you to process faith questions and progress with someone of a very similar life stage or experience? Why or why not?

Did you previously have distractions or obstacles in your spiritual life that you worked through or have outgrown?

PART 3:

Why You're More Ready Than You Think for Disciplemaking

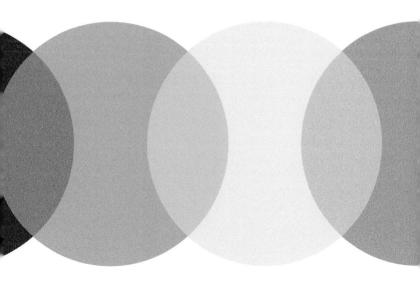

A Confidence Crisis

**Self-doubt gets in the way of disciplemaking—
but it doesn't have to**

Barna's research suggests there are many Christians who feel any-thing but confident when engaging in discipleship. Even if some-body understands the value of shared spiritual growth (as we covered in part one) and even if they create space for it in their lives (as we covered in part two), self-doubt can creep in.

Among Christians who aren't helping someone grow in their faith and move closer to Christ, the main reason is clear: not feel-ing qualified or equipped (37%). This response is selected far more than other issues like a lack of attention (22% haven't thought about it) or a lack of connection (24% say nobody has suggested it).

Self-doubt reveals itself again when we gauge interest in disciplemaking a different way. Among Christians who are not

Feeling Ill-Equipped Is the Top Reason Christians Do Not Make Disciples

You said you are not helping someone grow in their faith and move closer to Christ. Please select which item comes closest to describing why.

Don't think I am qualified / equipped	37%
No one has suggested it / asked me	24%
Just haven't thought about it	22%
Had a bad experience in the past	3%
Other	14%

n=1,643 U.S. Christian adults who are not disciplemakers, December 22, 2020–January 18, 2021.

interested in "intentionally helping people learn from and live more like Jesus," the top three reasons for their low interest all stem from not feeling they have what it takes in one way or another. One-third doesn't feel qualified to address hard topics (37%), doesn't think they would be very good at it (35%) or doesn't think they are knowledgeable enough about the Bible or Christianity (31%). Similarly, 24 percent assume this is a job fit for actual ministry professionals or church leaders, and one in four (28%) says they just don't know how to make disciples.

Elsewhere in our research, there are other signs of uncertainty or unease about discipleship relationships. Some Christians, especially younger ones, say they aren't being discipled because they

Top 5 Reasons Christians Are
Not Interested in Being a Disciplemaker

I don't feel qualified to address hard topics — 37%

I don't think I would be very good at it — 35%

I don't think I'm knowledgeable enough about the Bible or Christianity — 31%

I wouldn't know how to do it — 28%

This sounds like the job of a church leader or ministry professional — 24%

n=1,395 U.S. Christian adults who are "maybe" or "not" interested in becoming a disciplemaker, June 1–July 4, 2020.

don't know how to begin this kind of relationship with someone.

Interestingly, we see self-doubt decline as people embrace spiritual accountability and support for themselves. Specifically, among Christians who are being discipled but are not discipling others, the fear of not being qualified or equipped is less often seen as the hurdle to making disciples (29% vs. 42% of Christians with no discipleship community cite this reason). For this group, not having been asked to disciple someone (31%) is as much a hang-up as lack of confidence. The barriers shift from ability to opportunity. Is it possible that, because someone else is spiritually investing in them, they are becoming more prepared to boldly invest in others?

Comfort & Confidence

Ultimately, discipleship community doesn't require confidence.

Yes, it's true that disciplemaking does correlate with greater ease in things like talking about scripture with others (84% of those in discipleship community say they are comfortable doing so vs. 40% of those who aren't in discipleship community). But, as you'll see, even Christians who are engaged in discipleship community encounter friction in relationships (see page 109). Spiritual maturity doesn't necessarily stem from knowledge or self-assuredness; however, it is connected, at least in part, to a readiness to be vulnerable.

What might that look like? The majority of Christians in discipleship community feels comfortable walking through suffering or hardship with others (58% very comfortable, 36% somewhat comfortable) and makes a habit of confessing and talking through their sins or wrongdoings with a trusted friend (65% have done so

---

EVERYDAY DISCIPLEMAKERS ON ... FACING SELF-DOUBT

" I think sharing your faith is always a bit fraught with insecurity! I try to remind myself and others that it is God's movement, not my words, that really changes a heart. God is already engaging them in conversation whether they realize it or not. I urge people to listen and ask questions rather than try to preach."

" Are there situations with unbelievers where I am unsure what to say, or if I should say anything? Absolutely. I try to share based on scripture, and if that is the case, then I can be confident."

in the past year). These disciples and disciplemakers are owning up to wrongs and processing the toughest parts of life together with people they trust—not exactly activities that involve feeling wholly qualified and knowledgeable! But that openness may lead to greater confidence in one's relationship to God and to others, if not in oneself.

If friendship is fertile ground for discipleship, then vulnerability is critical in tending its soil. It's worrying, then, that **Christians are split on whether vulnerability is naturally present in their interactions with friends.** Just over half (54%) agree at least somewhat that it's easy for them to be vulnerable. (For context, among those in discipleship community, that percentage climbs to 66% compared to 42% of Christians who are outside discipleship community).

Thankfully, three-quarters of Christians overall (and even more among younger generations) say they have a Christian friend

❝ Giving people the space to share how it's been hard to share their faith and encouraging them in the small steps they've taken is good."

❝ I encourage others to look at how God has met them in the disciplines and the details of their lives. Those are the things he has given them to pass on … and sometimes he makes our feeble efforts highly effective and productive."

Trust, Openness & Discipleship Go Together

● All Christians ● In discipleship community
Only discipling others ● Only being discipled
● Not engaged in discipleship

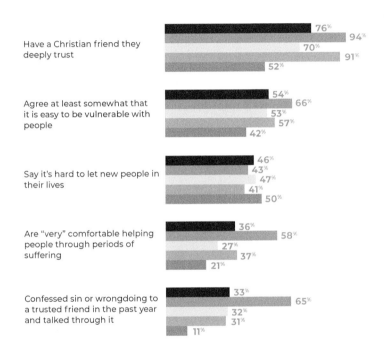

Have a Christian friend they
deeply trust
- 76%
- 94%
- 70%
- 91%
- 52%

Agree at least somewhat that
it is easy to be vulnerable with
people
- 54%
- 66%
- 53%
- 57%
- 42%

Say it's hard to let new people in
their lives
- 46%
- 43%
- 47%
- 41%
- 50%

Are "very" comfortable helping
people through periods of
suffering
- 36%
- 58%
- 27%
- 37%
- 21%

Confessed sin or wrongdoing to
a trusted friend in the past year
and talked through it
- 33%
- 65%
- 32%
- 31%
- 11%

n=2,511 U.S. Christian adults, December 22, 2020–January 18, 2021.

they trust. Nearly all Christians who are in discipleship community (94%) have this trusting connection—something only half of Christians who aren't engaged in discipleship (52%) experience.

That is both a warning sign and a starting point. Trust and vulnerability dovetail in the data. In fact, 85 percent of those who strongly agree that it is easy to be vulnerable with others also have a Christian friend they trust (compared to just 70% of those who admit to struggling with vulnerability). Additionally, vulnerable Christians are more than twice as likely to see it as a sign of health when friends challenge each other (66% vs. 24% strongly agree).

As we'll continue to see in this guide, active disciplemakers may still have low moments. Even as they lean into spiritual disciplines and growth, they still face fears and struggles in their relationships—the key word here, perhaps, being *in*. They stay *in* those close relationships, caring about their friends' growth in Christ and taking steps to bring them along on the way of Jesus.

Acknowledging what you don't know or where you come up short doesn't have to become a reason for delaying or avoiding discipleship community. The areas where you would like to be more equipped or knowledgeable reveal opportunities for growth *and* openness with people you trust.

A standout quality of discipleship community is embracing radical vulnerability, not having all the answers.

A Summary of Key Stats:

Thirty-seven percent of Christians who aren't helping someone grow in their faith and move closer to Christ say they are held back because they do not feel qualified or equipped.

Eighty-four percent of Christians in discipleship community are comfortable sharing what they have learned about the Bible with others.

Two-thirds of Christians in discipleship community have confessed sins or wrongdoings to a trusted friend in the past year, or say it's easy to be vulnerable with people.

Questions for Reflection:

What question or topic are you most worried about having to address in a discipleship context? What would it look like to have a healthy, open, judgment-free conversation about this?

As a disciple, what can you do to grow in knowledge *and* grow in vulnerability?

Who are your trusted friends? Are you vulnerable together, even about hard or embarrassing situations? Why or why not?

Questions to Ask Your Friends:

Is there something about Christianity or discipleship you wish you were more equipped to talk with people about? Would you be open to learning more about that together?

Can you recall a time you felt confident and comfortable talking about your faith or beliefs? What does that look like or feel like for you?

How could I be more helpful in processing life's hardships with you, or in talking through areas in which God is calling you to grow? Is it okay if I come to you to do the same?

That Awkward Moment When ...

It's OK to feel like a tongue-tied disciplemaker

Some Christians struggle to begin conversations about their faith because they worry it will seem abrupt, unnatural or too personal. Maybe you're one of these Christians. And it makes sense that you feel this way.

Letting someone into your life may be difficult on its own; in fact, about half of Christians (46%) say this is the case. Add to that broader cultural hesitations around Christianity, and it's not a surprise that you might sense social hurdles to sharing about your faith. For instance, the percentage of Americans who identify as "Christian" has declined 16 percent since 1990; meanwhile, one-quarter of U.S. adults (24%) now does not identify with any religious tradition. Young adults, especially, have their guard up with Christian institutions, with Millennials and Gen Z being less likely than their elders to believe the Church is good for people, creates peace or is important for society.

Still, Barna research suggests that spiritual curiosity persists, even in the absence of religious certainty or Christian identity. Christians shouldn't give up hope when it comes to talking about their personal faith with others, believers and non-believers alike. Consider that, especially in the Millennial and Gen Z generations, even non-Christians regularly talk about spiritual matters and express interest in learning more about Christianity.

Sharing one's faith with others is a critical piece of disciplemaking and relationship-building. There is simply no spiritual multiplication of Christianity without taking the leap—however clumsy it may be—to talk to others about following Jesus and about how much God loves them. Those who open themselves up to new or deepened friendships may find their halting conversations become a catalyst for exciting spiritual growth all around.

Discipling Through Differences

Let's look at some of the common relational gaps Christians often encounter. Perhaps these are tensions or struggles you have sensed yourself. If so, we hope this data will help you feel less alone and to see relational differences as opportunities to build bridges, not borders.

Engaging with People of Other Generations

Roughly one in four Christians (23%) struggles to engage with those from a different generation than their own.

The generational chasm appears wider from the vantage point of younger Christians. Nearly one-third of both Millennials (31%) and Gen Z (32%) admits a struggle to engage with people from different generations, while 22 percent of Gen X and just 16 percent of Boomers say the same thing.

Could you be missing out on a rich, natural source for spiritual mentorship by ruling out cross-generational relationships?

Engaging with People of Other Cultures

One-quarter of Christians (25%) struggles to engage with people of different cultures.

Younger generations have a more diverse ethnic makeup than older generations, and Barna has observed that people in younger generations tend to value welcoming people who are different from them. Perhaps this attentiveness leads to more awareness of differences; interestingly, younger adults are still more likely than older generations to say they struggle to engage with people outside of their own culture. Three in 10 Millennials (30%) and Gen Z (29%) feel this way. In contrast, only 22 percent of Boomers and 23 percent of Gen X report this struggle to interact across cultures.

Do you need to reframe interactions with people of different cultures as a fulfillment of loving one's neighbor and bearing witness to God's creativity?

Engaging with People of Other Faiths

Christians can seek to build disciples in many places, and this study shows they often find discipleship relationships among their peers through their church or spiritual communities. These relationships are important, allowing Christians to both teach and learn how to better obey and love Jesus. However, discipleship shouldn't be only an insular activity among believers. Instead, Jesus' disciples were told to make *new* disciples among those who didn't know him. Disciplemaking started with evangelism, and these activities of the Christian walk are still linked today. Sharing one's faith is an important part of developing one's spiritual life.

For many Christians, finding non-Christian friends isn't a problem. **Most Christians have relationships with people who don't share their faith.** In fact, more than half of Christians (58%) say they have at least one genuine friendship with someone who doesn't know Jesus.

But many Christians see the topic of faith as off-limits in their relationships with non-Christians. **One in four Christians (23%) says they are afraid to have spiritual conversations with people who aren't Christians.** Additionally, one in five Christians (20%) struggles to know how to relate to people outside their faith.

EVERYDAY DISCIPLEMAKERS ON ... **SPIRITUAL ICEBREAKERS**

" If we believe that God has put us together, and that we are both seeking to grow more like him, we can safely share a 10 minute 'testimony.' *What is different about your life because you know Jesus?*"

Younger generations are more likely to struggle with this; 30 percent of Gen Z and 28 percent of Millennials fear having faith conversations with non-Christians. Only one-fifth of Gen X (20%) and Boomers (22%) reports the same challenge. Similarly, younger Christian generations don't always know how to connect with non-Christians in the first place. More Gen Z (31%) and Millennials (27%) struggle to know how to relate to non-Christians, compared to 19 percent of Gen X and 12 percent of Boomers.

Christians in younger generations are more likely to have non-Christian friends, so they might be more aware of the challenges that can come from interacting with people of other faith traditions. Additionally, they may be staying away from faith-sharing in an effort to be considerate or avoid conflict; in a previous Barna study, two-thirds of Christian Millennials (65%) agreed that people today are more likely than in the past to take offense if they share their faith.

“ I think drilling into people's stories, hopes, dreams and disappointments is a great way to get into spiritual conversations with people. *What's something you're passionate about? What's something you've been learning about? Was there any spiritual background to your childhood?* [These] are great questions to ask.”

“ Conversations are so individual and moment-based. I think listening is the best starter, then asking questions, then sharing a personal story as a bridge or asking them to share a story on the subject.”

The research does point to something that might help Christians become more comfortable with non-Christians: putting in quality time. Just one-quarter of Christians (26%) spends meaningful time with non-Christians on a weekly basis. But the more that Christians do so, the less likely they are to feel afraid of having spiritual conversations. They are also more likely to feel comfortable sharing what they've learned about the Bible with others.

It's true that few non-Christians have interest in a one-on-one mentoring relationship with a Christian to pray, explore and discuss the Bible and share experiences of everyday life; 23 percent are "maybe" interested, just 7 percent "definitely" are. But those who *are* interested say it's because they are eager to learn (49%). And the number one way they want to explore their questions about Christianity, they say, is on an individual basis: **38 percent of non-Christians who are interested in discipleship mentoring say talking to someone they know who has a deep faith would be most useful for them.**

Don't count yourself out as a resource for your non-Christian friends or assume they don't want to talk about faith—they might welcome an opportunity to process insights and questions with you and may even see your friendship as their preferred space for learning about Christianity.

The Struggle Is Real—But Worth It

You may have noticed some patterns are emerging. When the average Christian encounters someone of a different experience, regardless of the dissimilarity, there's about a one-in-four chance they will face difficulty in their interactions. Among younger

Christians, who have bigger and more varied social circles, that chance increases.

This generational trend, however, is an example of a key lesson from the research: The sense of awkwardness in cross-generational, cross-cultural or cross-religious relationships *grows* in proximity and with practice. **The struggle to engage isn't overcome by being in relationship; it's often part of being in relationship.**

Let's check in with Christians who are actively in discipleship community. Looking across the spectrum of discipleship activity, the Christians who both receive and extend discipleship in relationship are most likely to say they struggle to interact with people across cultures or across age gaps and to face difficulty relating to or sharing faith with non-Christians. This isn't for lack of opportunity; after all, seven in 10 Christians in discipleship community have at least one genuine friendship with someone who doesn't know Jesus. One in three (34%) says they spend meaningful time with non-Christians on a weekly basis.

These are Christians who intentionally care for the spiritual lives of others. They seek and find opportunities to invest in their friends. They aren't always heads-down in their Bible or isolated in their prayer closets; they are engaged with others and with their world. We might reason that they are attuned to the occasional awkwardness or difficulty of discipleship *because* of their intentional and regular exposure to it.

Following their example, you may want to consider the people you spend time with, and be open to building relationships with people of different backgrounds. These bonds can give you new perspectives and wisdom, nurture curiosity and humility and provide an excellent forum to be a witness of God's love. Embrace the

Disciplemaking Means Engaging Across Differences (Even When It's a Struggle)

% say "yes"

● All Christians ● In discipleship community
○ Only discipling others ● Only being discipled
● Not engaged in discipleship

Have at least one genuine friendship with someone who doesn't know Jesus
- 58%
- 70%
- 58%
- 59%
- 48%

Afraid to have spiritual conversations with non-Christians
- 23%
- 27%
- 20%
- 19%
- 24%

Struggle knowing how to relate to non-Christians
- 20%
- 32%
- 24%
- 16%
- 12%

Struggle to engage with people from different cultures
- 25%
- 33%
- 28%
- 22%
- 22%

Struggle to engage with people from different generations
- 23%
- 31%
- 27%
- 21%
- 18%

n=2,511 U.S. Christian adults, December 22, 2020–January 18, 2021.

challenge to grow in healthy ways, which the majority of Christians says is a mark of friendship.

Don't be discouraged if engaging with others, especially in spiritual conversations or practices, is awkward or fumbling at times. You're not alone with these challenges, and you may be more ready than you think to engage. Allow your unease to keep you sharp, honest and considerate. Share generously and authentically about what you believe and practice. Be honest about what you don't know or what you wrestle with. Ask questions with compassion and a listening ear.

A fruitful conversation doesn't always have to be a smooth one.

A Summary of Key Stats:

About one-quarter of Christians struggles to engage with people from other cultures, other generations or other faiths.

The likelihood of acknowledging the difficulty of connecting across differences actually *increases* for people who experience regular and diverse community; about one-third of Christians who are engaged in discipleship community feels this way.

Half of non-Christians who are interested in a discipleship mentor are simply eager to learn. Two-fifths would like to do so in their individual relationships with people of faith.

Questions for Reflection:

When do you feel awkward or uncomfortable socially? How can you be an authentic, loving and persistent presence even in these situations?

Do you have genuine friendships with people who don't know Jesus? How often do you spend time with them?

Have you ever been accepted or embraced even though you were very different from a person or a group? What was that like? Did it teach you anything about faith?

Questions to Ask Your Friends:

Do you have difficulty letting new people into your life? How often do you have opportunity to do so? Do you wish it happened more often?

What is most important to you to have in common with people? What differences do you seek out or welcome?

(If your friend is a non-Christian) Is there anything about my personal faith or about Christianity in general that you are curious about?

Start Where You Are

**The best people to journey with could be
the people already around you**

Modeling meaningful relationships with others is a powerful witness to God's love. Likewise, community of all kinds—Christian groups, family, friends, neighbors and coworkers—can encourage you through your struggles and victories. Growing in confidence as a disciple and disciplemaker involves seeing the potential in relationships and seizing those opportunities.

Hopefully, by this point in *Growing Together*, you're convinced of the impact of discipleship. You see that it's vital and, encouragingly, it's possible. You want to organize your spiritual life, your routines and your relationships toward the multiplication of Christ-followers. So, you wonder: *Where should I begin to meet and reach people?*

Start by looking around. Bonds and friendships from your daily life can be foundations for belonging, support and boldness. Do you know other believers who value growing in their walk with Jesus? Do you know people who may have never truly heard the Christian gospel? How might you link arms?

Four Postures of Potential Disciples

There may not be one profile for the "right" relationship to invest in or a secret to finding it, but **there is some common ground on which potential disciples and disciplemakers tend to gather.**

In preliminary research for this study, Barna observed some characteristics that act like basic building blocks for discipleship relationships. As you seek to disciple others, you may find enthusiastic company in people who have the following attributes.

These attitudes are not explicitly spiritual or unique to "churchy" crowds. Rather, these forward-thinking qualities and convictions tend to go together with an openness to spiritual growth. They are the postures of people—Christians *and* non-Christians—who are hungry for more, working on themselves and, accordingly, more likely to see value in discipleship if it is offered to them. Take some time to reflect on the postures of those you surround yourself with, or even of those you are considering discipling. Do they possess these qualities?

Prayerfully evaluate yourself as you read, as well. Do you lack any of these attributes? How could you develop in these areas? Who do you trust to encourage you to grow in these ways?

SEEK OUT PEOPLE WHO ARE OPTIMISTIC FOR CHANGE

People who are optimistic for change are convicted by their daily ability to impact the world and those immediately around them. We see this in their belief that their life and actions make a difference. They focus on positively impacting those around them, and they believe every day is an opportunity to grow. They agree that their life has a meaningful impact on the world.

SEEK OUT PEOPLE WHO ARE ACCOUNTABILITY-DRIVEN

Adults driven by accountability know the importance of mentorship and give others the authority to lead them in various areas of their lives. They believe the best way to grow or change is to have accountability with another person, and thus value having a mentor, advisor or coach to help facilitate that growth or change. This might be someone who values a personal trainer or coach more than individual workouts, or someone who seeks out a financial advisor. This group looks for leaders to invest in them and, likewise, invests in the growth of younger people.

SEEK OUT PEOPLE WHO ARE RELATIONALLY MOTIVATED

Being relationally motivated means feeling bound to friends' growth and sharing what you have been given. People in this category are motivated to make an impact on others and invested in the growth of those they feel close to. They agree, "The more I grow personally, the more I can help others grow." In turn, they say their friends care about and contribute to their growth.

SEEK OUT PEOPLE WHO ARE GROWTH-MINDED

Adults who are growth-minded know there is always more work to do, and they seek opportunities to challenge themselves in various parts of their lives. Sixty percent of those who qualify as

Four Groups Looking for Something More

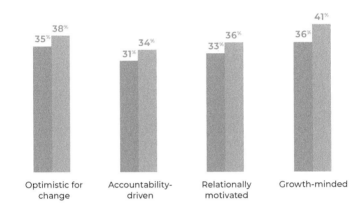

● All U.S. adults ● U.S. Christians

Optimistic for change: 35%, 38%
Accountability-driven: 31%, 34%
Relationally motivated: 33%, 36%
Growth-minded: 36%, 41%

n=2,930 U.S. adults, June 1–July 4, 2020.

EVERYDAY DISCIPLEMAKERS ON … CREATING SPACES TO SHARE

❝ Connecting and building relationships of trust is a very important part of the discipleship relationship. Inviting someone over for dinner, allowing them to see you in your relationship with your partner, kids, work and daily life is important."

❝ If a disciple does not experience a community of grace (a safe place to share), they will never discuss the deeper things of the heart that are needed for disciples to grow."

growth-minded report experiencing vibrant spiritual growth in the past year (compared to 27% of all U.S. adults). An additional 29 percent say they spiritually grew some but wish they had experienced even *more* growth (vs. 12%). Accordingly, they are hopeful for and committed to investing in their spiritual growth.

A 2020 Barna survey, commissioned by The Navigators, defined disciplemaking as intentionally helping people learn from and live more like Jesus by praying with them, studying the Bible together and sharing in experiences of everyday life. A disciplemaker, then, is someone who invests time with a Christian who is new to faith or with a non-Christian who is interested in faith, with the goal of inspiring and equipping them to then go and do the same with others. In this way, the number of disciples grows, and disciplemakers are strengthened in their own faith. Christians were asked if they had interest in being a discipleship mentor, while non-Christians were asked if they had interest in having a discipleship mentor.

❝ It is easier to be vulnerable if you can also spend some of your time together engaging in shared interests and just hanging out, rather than only meeting to do activities focused specifically on discipleship. It helps to get to know each other as people as well."

❝ Asking a friend to dinner, hearing their story, inviting them into my life, sharing my heart are all important steps on the discipleship journey."

Desire for General Growth Links to Interest in Discipleship

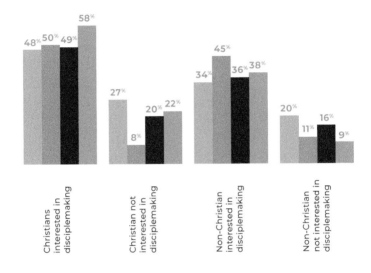

⬤ Optimistic for Change ⬤ Accountability Driven
⬤ Relationally Motivated ⬤ Growth-minded

n=2,930 U.S. adults, June 1–July 4, 2020.

Overall, similar proportions of all U.S. adults, including Christians, have these qualities and they are relatively consistent across age groups. Across the board—among both Christians and non-Christians—adults who fall into these groups are more likely to express interest in discipleship community. Additionally, the more of these groups someone falls into, the more interest they likely have in discipleship.

In other words, no matter where you land spiritually, you might land on this common ground of wanting more for your life, for your development and for your community. Further, the inclination toward these four areas of personal growth has a powerful relationship to interest in disciplemaking, at times more so than starting from a particular faith affiliation or point of view.

What does this mean for a disciplemaker? The door to meaningful spiritual conversations and spiritual growth is wider than you think. Invitations to discipleship community don't need to be formal; they can be personal, relatable and authentic. They don't need to come from someone who has "already arrived"; they can arise between people who'd like to journey through everyday life together. They aren't exclusive to "spiritual" environments, and they not only help us grow closer to Jesus, they also nurture the daily and deeply human desires to change, learn and share.

Develop Relationships Where You Live & Work

Close relationships are foundational to feeling empowered for discipleship, and they can create a space for much-needed rest and refreshment. Additionally, healthy, life-to-life relationships with non-Christians can be an antidote to the negative assumptions some people have about followers of Jesus.

Classrooms, sidewalks, parks, gyms, offices, Zoom calls and all the daily spaces of our lives are wonderful places for Christians to cultivate closeness and bear witness to the gospel in practical, consistent ways.

The workplace especially promotes consistent connection. About half of employed Christians (51%) say they know what's going on in the lives of their coworkers, and this proportion increases among Christians who are giving and receiving discipleship in their relationships (62% vs. 41% of Christians not engaged in discipleship).

By comparison, only one-quarter of Christians (27%) knows what's going on in the lives of their neighbors. **In this data lies a call to better relational work-life balance, or at least increased intentionality in the arena that lies between the office and the home.** Even in an era that tends to over-schedule, disciples and disciplemakers are more present locally and more likely to report connection and communication with neighbors (45% vs. 19% of Christians not engaged in discipleship).

Some ages and stages of life are prone to be plugged into community. For example, younger Christians or Christians who are raising kids seem to have deeper (or at least more frequent) connections with their neighbors and colleagues.

Regardless of the nature of these individual interactions, we see that disciples who are experiencing strong growth in Christ demonstrate rootedness in community and a mindfulness of others.

Do you stay open to building relationships with the people you interact with regularly? What limits, self-imposed or otherwise, keep you from everyday connections? Do you have any ties where you live and work that God might be calling you to strengthen?

Balance Family & Non-Family Investments Wisely

Christians rightly care about their families and the faith formation of their children, siblings and other relatives. For many, family is the primary focus when it comes to investing in the spiritual growth of others. In fact, nearly three-quarters of Christians (72%) agree, three in 10 strongly so (29%), that investing time in the spiritual growth of their family is their primary focus.

Disciplemakers Seek Out Daily Connections

% say "yes"

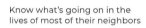

● All Christians ● In discipleship community
Only discipling others ● Only being discipled
● Not engaged in discipleship

Know what's going on in the
lives of most of their neighbors

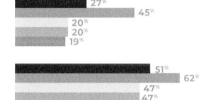

27%
45%
20%
20%
19%

Know what's going on in the
lives of their coworkers *

51%
62%
47%
47%
41%

n=2,511 U.S. Christian adults, December 22, 2020–January 18, 2021.
*among employed Christians

This investment is often fruitful and shouldn't be neglected. Barna research attests to the enduring value of being in a household that is hospitable, interactive and focused on spiritual growth. Parents and guardians especially can be an invaluable spiritual resource for their children, and they will often need to spend significant time and energy raising and discipling their kids. The home is a natural, sacred place to incorporate prayer, Bible study and spiritual conversation.

Disciplemaking in the home can potentially have ripple effects that extend well beyond family. Yet only one in six Christians (16%) strongly agrees that investing in the spiritual growth of people *other than family members* is a priority to them. All

Disciplemakers Focus on the Family

"When it comes to investing time in the spiritual growth of others,
my family and extended family are my primary focus."

● Strongly agree ● Somewhat agree
● Somewhat disagree ● Strongly disagree

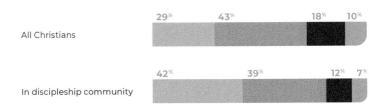

All Christians

29%   43%   18%   10%

In discipleship community

42%   39%   12%   7%

...But Also Spiritually Invest in Non-Family

"Investing in the spiritual growth of people other
than family members is a priority in my life."

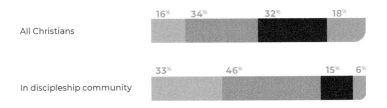

All Christians

16%   34%   32%   18%

In discipleship community

33%   46%   15%   6%

n=2,511 U.S. Christian adults, December 22, 2020–January 18, 2021.

told, Christians are evenly split on whether this is a personal priority (50% agree at least somewhat, 50% disagree at least somewhat).

Some conditions boost the priority of discipleship outside the family, such as spending meaningful time with non-Christians or feeling a responsibility to invest in others. Christians who are engaged in discipleship are more likely to report these mindsets, so it's not surprising they are also more likely to strongly agree that they aim to spiritually invest in non–family members (33% vs. 5% who are not engaged in discipleship), as well as their family.

Do you struggle to prioritize relationships with family or non–family members? Do you need to reinvest in the spiritual growth of those either inside or outside your home? Talk about it with someone you consider to be a discipleship mentor. Seek wisdom from believers you know who balance strong relationships at home, at work and at church. Ask them how they manage their time and energy and how they incorporate God's leading into that decision-making.

The beauty of true discipleship community is that the calling of the Christian life is shared. No one person bears the weight of leading, mentoring or seeking Jesus. Rather, people come together in regular community, practicing reciprocal and cyclical ways to draw closer to God and to one another, strengthening each other for their many other responsibilities and relationships.

A Summary of Key Stats:

People who are optimistic for change, accountability-driven, relationally motivated or growth-minded also tend to be open to being or having a discipleship mentor.

Christians who are engaged in discipleship community know what's going on with their neighbors (45%) and coworkers (62%).

Christians who are engaged in discipleship community value non-family discipleship (33% strongly agree they spiritually invest in non-family relationships), in addition to their primary focus on family discipleship (42%).

Questions for Reflection:

Based on the definitions that begin on page 114, do you see yourself as being optimistic for change? Accountability-driven? Relationally motivated? Growth-minded?

Do you feel attuned to the spiritual potential of relationships in the spaces you daily occupy—in your work, school, home or neighborhood?

How do you steward your spiritual investment or discipleship relationships inside and outside your household?

Questions to Ask Your Friends:

Do you ever feel God moving in small daily moments—conversations with a neighbor, a meeting with a coworker, an interaction online? If so, can you tell me more about a time you sensed this?

Are there people you are close to with whom you have never talked about your personal faith? If so, why not?

Do you have a family member who has made a strong impact on your spiritual growth? A non-family member? What did they do that encouraged you?

How We've Grown Already

However you came across this guide, Barna Group and The Navigators pray that *Growing Together* inspired you to grow in Christ and help others do the same.

Let's look back on what we've learned along the way.

First, we focused on why disciplemaking matters at all. It's not just nice to have; it's a calling that can transform your life and the lives of those around you. We examined some of the spiritual and social benefits of growing in Christ with others and were reminded that faith isn't meant to be entirely private. Since the first disciples, Christians have been intentionally partnering with friends and loved ones in their efforts to follow Jesus.

Then, we looked at the very real (but by no means insurmountable!) challenges to day-to-day discipleship. We learned from disciplemakers who steward their hours and energy in a way that allows for meaningful time committed to growing in faith and sharing life with others. We even zoomed in to provide practical tips about how to make discipleship happen in various seasons when you may wonder what you are able to give.

Finally, we confronted sources of insecurity, awkwardness or reservation that can hold people back from the rich, life-giving realities of disciplemaking. Both the research and the personal stories of disciplemakers offered this encouragement: Confidence may grow with time, practice and mentorship—*but you have what you need to begin to lean into discipleship community today.* You have the comfort and guidance of the Holy Spirit, you have the ability to be vulnerable with others, and you have various relationships within which God can move.

Your "readiness" depends on your willingness to take the next step. And then the next one. And then the next one.

Most importantly, as you seek to fulfill the Great Commission to make disciples, rely on the Great Commandment as well:

"Love the Lord your God with all your heart and with all your soul and with all your mind and with all your strength. ... Love your neighbor as yourself. There is no commandment greater than these." (Mark 12:30–31).

Continuing the Journey

Barna Group and The Navigators previously partnered on a 2015 study and report called *The State of Discipleship*. Prepared for church leaders exploring discipleship models, it provides a comprehensive look at how to foster and measure transformative discipleship. You can purchase this report at **shop.barna.com** or receive it in Barna Access.

Barna Access is a subscription-based service that offers a wealth of relevant data, knowledge from faith leaders and timely cultural insights for your context anytime, anywhere. Get every Barna report, and more, all in one place. **barnaaccess.com**

The Navigators designed a Digital Discipleship Journey™ email series to inspire and equip you to grow in Christ and help others do the same. Start your free Digital Discipleship Journey at **navigators.org/disciplemaking**.

How to Save the World: Disciplemaking Made Simple, written by Alice Matagora and published by NavPress, will empower you on your disciplemaking journey, helping you break down barriers and discover practical ways to participate in God's redemptive work in the world. **Available early summer 2022 at NavPress.com.**

Pointers for Reading Data

Growing Together is grounded in Barna research, which means you'll encounter data and statistics both in the text and in charts. Here are a few things to keep in mind to make sense of the numbers and help turn research into action in your own life.

It's important to know the context of a survey—when it was conducted, how and among whom. We've summarized those details for you below, in the Methodology. You'll also catch brief summaries of this information throughout the book. (For example, when you see "*n*=2,511 U.S. Christian adults, December 22, 2020–January 18, 2021," below a chart, that means the corresponding data is from a sample of 2,511 U.S. adults who are Christians, conducted within the date range mentioned.) Charts will include all relevant context, such as the question text, legends and labels for multiple groups or multiple responses and, if needed, details about the base when it is smaller than the total sample.

Many times, we'll also include percentages within parentheses. Upon first mention or in the surrounding text, we'll note which groups are being represented or compared by those percentages or what response they gave.

Methodology

This quantitative study consisted of two online surveys. First, an online survey was conducted among 2,511 adults who self-identify as Christian and live within the United States. The adults who completed this survey were randomly selected through online research panels. This survey was conducted from December 22, 2020 to January 18, 2021. The margin of error for the data is +/- 1.8 percent at the 95 percent confidence level, meaning Barna researchers are 95 percent confident that the true national numbers lie within this small margin of error.

Second, an online survey of 2,930 U.S. adults was conducted from June 1 to July 4, 2020. The margin of error for this data is +/- 1.5 percent at the 95 percent confidence level.

As you read this report, take into consideration that the data was collected during the COVID-19 pandemic.

In quantitative research, it is important to ensure that the data is balanced and doesn't favor one people group over another. To accomplish this, researchers set quotas and tracked a variety of demographic factors as the data came in. They carefully managed the balance of region, ethnicity, education, age and gender in particular (i.e., applied "weights" to the data set) to ensure that the data reflected these demographics' natural presence in the American population (using U.S. Census Bureau data for comparison). Partly by nature of using an online panel, these respondents are slightly more educated than the average, but Barna researchers made sure that the voices of those without college degrees were appropriately represented in the final set of data.

Key Terms

Gen Z were born 1999 to 2015. Only adults 18 or older are included in this data set.

Millennials were born 1984 to 1998.

Gen X were born 1965 to 1983.

Boomers were born 1946 to 1964.

Barna Group categorized respondents in our survey to zoom in on and better understand the relationships that support spiritual growth. These profiles appear throughout *Growing Together*.

To qualify as being discipled, or being in a discipleship relationship, a Christian respondent must:

Say they have a relationship with another Christian (other than a family member) who provides accountability, encouragement and support and with whom they help each other grow spiritually

To qualify as discipling others, or being a disciplemaker, a Christian respondent must:

Say they currently are actively helping someone to grow in their faith and move closer to Christ

To qualify as being in discipleship community, a Christian respondent experiences both relationship dynamics above.

A 2020 Barna survey, commissioned by The Navigators, defined disciplemaking as: intentionally helping people learn from and live more like Jesus by praying with them, studying the Bible together and sharing in experiences of everyday life. A disciple-maker, then, is someone who invests time with a Christian who is new to faith or with a non-Christian who is interested in faith, with the goal of inspiring and equipping them to do the same with others. In this way, the number of disciples grows, and disciple-makers are strengthened in their own faith.

Acknowledgments

Barna Group is grateful to continue partnering with The Navigators to better understand and support present-day discipleship. Thanks to Amanda Trautmann and Stephanie Rich for being wonderful collaborators in this project and for your commitment to the spiritual growth of the everyday Christian.

Barna and The Navigators engaged a panel of everyday disciples and disciplemakers who generously provided quotes and insights we are honored to feature in these pages. This group includes the following names and several others who wished to be anonymous: Morna Comeau, Kyle Copeland, Amanda Ghilardi, J. Alasdair Groves, Jacqueline Holland, Bob Kuecker and Harry L. Saunders Jr.

Thanks to Patriece Johnson for kicking off this book so thoughtfully.

The research and analysis team for this study included Daniel Copeland, Pam Jacob, Savannah Kimberlin, David Kinnaman and Traci Stark. Alyce Youngblood and Kevin Singer produced the manuscript. Lauren Petersen and Layla Shahmohammadi coordinated the panel of disciplemakers. Doug Brown copy edited the manuscript. Annette Allen designed the book. With creative direction from Joe Jensen, OX Creative designed the cover. Brenda Usery managed production with project management assistance from Elissa Clouse and T'nea Rolle. The project team thanks our Barna colleagues Cicely Corry, Aidan Dunn, Ashley Ekmay, Mel Grabendike, Brooke Hempell, Dr. Charlotte Marshall Powell, Steve McBeth, Matt Randerson, Chanté Smith, Verónica Thames and Todd White.

Knowledge to Lead with Confidence in Your Church and in Your Home

The State of Discipleship
In the Great Commission, Jesus commanded his followers to make disciples. Learn about what is effective and get insights from churches that exemplify excellence in discipleship.

Gifted for More
Every Christian has specific gifts— unique skills, talents and abilities. In order for the Church to flourish and grow, individual Christians need to understand their gifts and use them well in daily life. This report is a great starting point.

Spiritual Conversations in the Digital Age
Go and tell . . . but how? The ways Christians share their faith, how often they engage in spiritual conversations and their goals during these exchanges have changed.

Reviving Evangelism in the Next Generation
The Church will be shaped by the attitudes and approaches young people bring to evangelism. Find out what the future may hold—and how Gen Z is beginning to step into a life of discipleship with their peers.

AVAILABLE AT BARNA.COM/RESOURCES